Practice*Planners*®

Arthur E. Jongsma, Jr., Series Editor

Helping therapists help their clients . . .

D1261719

Practice*Planners*

Second Edition

THE COMPLETE ADULT
PSYCHOTHERAPY
Treatment Planner

A new, fully revised edition of the bestselling *The Complete Psychotherapy Treatment Planner*, this invaluable resource features:

- Treatment plan components for 39 behaviorally based presenting problems—including two completely new problem sets

- A step-by-step guide to writing treatment plans

- Over 490 additional prewritten treatment goals, objectives, and interventions

- Handy workbook format with space to record your own treatment plan options

- Over 160,000 **Practice*Planners*** sold

Arthur E. Jongsma, Jr., and L. Mark Peterson

Practice*Planners*

Arthur E. Jongsma, Jr., Series Editor

Brief Therapy
HOMEWORK
PLANNER

- Contains 62 ready-to-copy homework assignments that can be used to facilitate brief individual therapy

- Homework assignments and exercises are keyed to over 39 behaviorally-based presenting problems from *The Complete Psychotherapy Treatment Planner*

- Assignments may be quickly customized using the enclosed disk

- Over 160,000 **Practice*Planners*** sold

Gary M. Schultheis

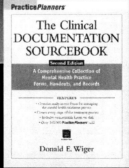

Practice*Planners*®

The Clinical
DOCUMENTATION
SOURCEBOOK

Second Edition

A Comprehensive Collection of
Mental Health Practice
Forms, Handouts, and Records

·········· FEATURES ··········

- Question marks-to-text forms for managing the mental health treatment process
- Covers every stage of the treatment process
- Includes reproducible forms on disk
- Over 160,000 **Practice*Planners*** sold

Donald E. Wiger

Practice*Planners*

Arthur E. Jongsma, Jr., Series Editor

The Adult Psychotherapy
PROGRESS NOTES PLANNER

This time-saving resource:

- Provides prewritten progress notes ready for the corresponding treatment problems

- Covers the gamut of disorder evaluations for every intervention suggested in the bestselling *Complete Adult Psychotherapy Treatment Planner* and others

- Includes 1,000s of clear statements describing client presentations and appropriate interventions descriptions

- Provides a handy workbook format for easier to record your own progress note options

- Over 160,000 **Practice*Planners*** sold

Arthur E. Jongsma, Jr.

⟨W⟩WILEY

Practice*Planners*® Order Form

Treatment Planners cover all the necessary elements for developing formal treatment plans, including detailed problem definitions, long-term goals, short-term objectives, therapeutic interventions, and DSM-IV diagnoses.

Documentation Sourcebooks provide a comprehensive collection of ready-to-use blank forms, handouts, and questionnaires to help you manage your client reports and streamline the record keeping and treatment process. Features clear, concise explanations of the purpose of each form—including when it should be used and at what point. Includes customizable forms on disk.

The Complete Adult Psychotherapy Treatment Planner, Second Edition
0-471-31924-4 / $44.95

The Child Psychotherapy Treatment Planner, Second Edition
0-471-34764-7 / $44.95

The Adolescent Psychotherapy Treatment Planner, Second Edition
0-471-34766-3 / $44.95

The Chemical Dependence Treatment Planner
0-471-23795-7 / $44.95

The Continuum of Care Treatment Planner
0-471-19568-5 / $44.95

The Couples Psychotherapy Treatment Planner
0-471-24711-1 / $44.95

The Employee Assistance (EAP) Treatment Planner
0-471-24709-X / $44.95

The Pastoral Counseling Treatment Planner
0-471-25416-9 / $44.95

The Older Adult Psychotherapy Treatment Planner
0-471-29574-4 / $44.95

The Behavioral Medicine Treatment Planner
0-471-31923-6 / $44.95

The Group Therapy Treatment Planner
0-471-37449-0 / $44.95

The Family Therapy Treatment Planner
0-471-34768-X / $44.95

The Severe and Persistent Mental Illness Treatment Planner
0-471-35945-9 / $44.95

The Gay and Lesbian Psychotherapy Treatment Planner
0-471-35080-X / $44.95

The Clinical Documentation Sourcebook, Second Edition
0-471-32692-5 / $49.95

The Psychotherapy Documentation Primer
0-471-28990-6 / $45.00

The Couple and Family Clinical Documentation Sourcebook
0-471-25234-4 / $49.95

The Clinical Child Documentation Sourcebook
0-471-29111-0 / $49.95

The Chemical Dependence Treatment Documentation Sourcebook
0-471-31285-1 / $49.95

The Forensic Documentation Sourcebook
0-471-25459-2 / $85.00

The Continuum of Care Clinical Documentation Sourcebook
0-471-34581-4 / $75.00

NEW AND FORTHCOMING

The Traumatic Events Treatment Planner
0-471-39587-0 / $44.95

The Special Education Treatment Planner
0-471-38873-4 / $44.95

The Mental Retardation and Developmental Disability Treatment Planner
0-471-38253-1 / $44.95

The Social Work and Human Services Treatment Planner
0-471-37741-4 / $44.95

The Rehabilitation Psychology Treatment Planner
0-471-35178-4 / $44.95

Name_____

Affiliation_____

Address_____

City/State/Zip_____

Phone/Fax_____

E-mail_____

www.wiley.com/practiceplanners

To order, call 1-800-753-0655
(Please refer to promo #1-4019 when ordering.)
Or send this page with payment* to:
John Wiley & Sons, Inc., Attn: J. Knott
605 Third Avenue, New York, NY 10158-0012

☐ Check enclosed   ☐ Visa   ☐ MasterCard   ☐ American Express

Card #_____

Expiration Date_____

Signature_____
*Please add your local sales tax to all orders.

Practice Management Tools for Busy Mental Health Professionals

Homework Planners feature dozens of behaviorally based, ready-to-use assignments that are designed for use between sessions, as well as a disk (Microsoft Word) containing all of the assignments—allowing you to customize them to suit your unique client needs.

Brief Therapy Homework Planner
0-471-24611-5 / $49.95

Brief Couples Therapy Homework Planner
0-471-29511-6 / $49.95

Brief Child Therapy Homework Planner
0-471-32366-7 / $49.95

Brief Adolescent Therapy Homework Planner
0-471-34465-6 / $49.95

Chemical Dependence Treatment Homework Planner
0-471-32452-3 / $49.95

Brief Employee Assistance Homework Planner
0-471-38088-1 / $49.95

Brief Family Therapy Homework Planner
0-471-385123-1 / $49.95

EW IN THE PRACTICE*PLANNERS*™ SERIES

Progress Notes Planners contain complete prewritten progress notes for each presenting problem in the companion *Treatment Planners*.

The Adult Psychotherapy Progress Notes Planner
0-471-34763-9 / $44.95

The Adolescent Psychotherapy Progress Notes Planner
0-471-38104-7 / $44.95

The Child Psychotherapy Progress Notes Planner
0-471-38102-0 / $44.95

To order by phone, call TOLL FREE 1-800-753-0655

Or contact us at:
John Wiley & Sons, Inc., Attn: J. Knott
605 Third Avenue, New York, NY 10158-0012
Fax: 1-800-597-3299
Online: www.wiley.com/practiceplanners

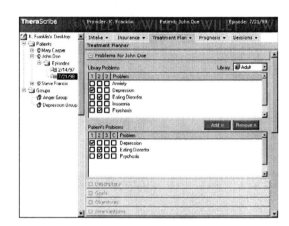

The Social Work and Human Services Treatment Planner

Practice *Planners*®

Arthur E. Jongsma, Jr., Series Editor

The Social Work and Human Services Treatment Planner

John S. Wodarski

Lisa Rapp-Paglicci

Catherine N. Dulmus

Arthur E. Jongsma, Jr.

JOHN WILEY & SONS, INC.

New York • Chichester • Weinheim • Brisbane • Singapore • Toronto

Note about Photocopy Rights

The publisher grants purchasers permission to reproduce handouts from this book for professional use with their clients.

Library of Congress Cataloging-in-Publication Data:
The social work and human services treatment planner / John S. Wodarski . . . [et al.].
    p. cm.—(Practice planners series)
    ISBN 978-0-471-37741-2
    1. Psychiatric social work—Planning. 2. Social case work—Planning. 3. Social service—Planning. I. Wodarski, John S. II. Practice planners
    HV689 .S63 2000
    361.3′2—dc21   00-043454

10 9 8 7 6 5 4 3 2 1

CONTENTS

SERIES PREFACE

The practice of psychotherapy has a dimension that did not exist 30, 20, or even 15 years ago—accountability. Treatment programs, public agencies, clinics, and even group and solo practitioners must now justify the treatment of patients to outside review entities that control the payment of fees. This development has resulted in an explosion of paperwork.

Clinicians must now document what has been done in treatment, what is planned for the future, and what the anticipated outcomes of the interventions are. The books and software in this Practice Planners series are designed to help practitioners fulfill these documentation requirements efficiently and professionally.

The Practice *Planners®* series is growing rapidly. It now includes not only the second editions of the *Complete Adult Psychotherapy Treatment Planner,* the *Child Psychotherapy Treatment Planner,* and the *Adolescent Psychotherapy Treatment Planner,* but also Treatment Planners targeted to specialty areas of practice, including chemical dependency, the continuum of care, couples therapy, employee assistance, behavioral medicine, therapy with older adults, pastoral counseling, family therapy, group therapy, social work and human services, therapy with gays and lesbians, and more.

In addition to the Treatment Planners, the series also includes Thera*Scribe®,* the latest version of the popular treatment planning and patient record-keeping software—as well as adjunctive books, such as the *Brief, Chemical Dependence, Couple, Child,* and *Adolescent Therapy Homework Planners;* the *Psychotherapy Documentation Primer;* and the *Clinical, Forensic, Child, Couple and Family, Continuum of Care,* and *Chemical Dependence Documentation Sourcebooks*—containing forms and resources to aid in mental health practice management. The most recent addition to this series is Progress Notes Planners for adolescents, children, and adults, respectively. The goal of the series is to provide practitioners with the resources they need in order to provide high-quality care in the era of accountability—or, to put it simply, we seek to help you spend more time on patients, and less on paperwork.

—ARTHUR E. JONGSMA, JR.

To my wife, Lois Ann Wodarski.

—John S. Wodarski

To David and Emily Ann, who have contributed more to my life than I could ever express.

—Lisa Rapp-Paglicci

For my aunts, Kandy Henely and Alisa-Paris Miller, with much love and admiration.

—Catherine N. Dulmus

To Larry Slager, a compassionate social worker and a valued friend, who continues to teach me to understand and embrace human diversity.

—Arthur E. Jongsma, Jr.

INTRODUCTION

Formalized treatment planning, which began in the medical sector in the 1960s, has become an integral component of mental health service delivery in the 1990s. To meet Joint Commission on Accreditation of Healthcare Organizations (JCAHO) standards, and help clients qualify for third-party reimbursement, treatment plans must be specific as to goal selection, problem definition, objective specification, and intervention implementation. The treatment plan must be individualized to meet the client's needs and goals and measurable in terms of setting milestones that can be used to chart the client's progress.

Although they are now a necessity, many clinicians lack formal training in the development of treatment plans. This is one area that most graduate school training programs fail to address, which often leaves the student at a disadvantage when embarking on clinical practice. The purpose of the *Social Work and Human Services Treatment Planner* is to clarify, simplify, improve, and accelerate the treatment planning process and to effectively deal with some of the hurdles that come with obtaining third-party authorization. It is also designed to serve as a framework for clinicians to follow as they plot an effective course of treatment with challenging cases.

TREATMENT PLAN UTILITY

Detailed written treatment plans can be beneficial to clients, the clinician, the treatment team, the insurance community, treatment agencies, and the overall mental health profession. The clients are served by a written plan which clearly delineates the issues that are the focus of treatment. It is very easy for both the clinician and the clients to lose sight of the issues that initially brought the clients into treatment. The treatment plan is a guide that structures the focus of the therapeutic contract and hopefully will help the clinician remain on track. Since issues can change as treatment progresses, the treatment plan must be viewed as a dynamic schematic or "road map" that can, and must, be updated to reflect any major change of problem, definition, goal, objective, or intervention. It also serves as a tracking system for clinicians to use when attempting to explain periods of impasse during the process of treatment.

Recognizing that the plan will in most cases continue to evolve throughout the treatment process, it remains important to settle on initial treatment goals at the outset. Behaviorally based, measurable objectives clearly focus the treatment endeavor and provide a means of assessing treatment outcome. Clear objectives also allow clients to channel their efforts into specific changes that will lead to the long-term goal of conflict resolution and healthy interaction.

Clinicians are aided by treatment plans because they are forced to think analytically, and critically, about which interventions are best suited for objective attainment for their clients. In multiprovider settings, treatment plans are not only designed to help clarify objectives, but also serve the important function of delineating which clinician is responsible for what interventions. By providing a common language, the *Social Work and Human Services Treatment Planner* can ensure consistent and clear communication among members of the treatment team.

Good communication improves quality of care and mitigates risk to the clinician. Malpractice suits are unfortunately increasing in frequency, and insurance premiums are consequently soaring. The first line of defense against allegations of malpractice is a complete clinical record detailing the treatment process. A written, customized, formal treatment plan that has been reviewed and signed by the clients, coupled with problem-oriented progress notes, is a powerful defense against false claims.

Every treatment agency or institution is constantly looking for ways to increase the quality and uniformity of the documentation in the clinical record. The demand for accountability from third-party payers and health maintenance organizations (HMOs) is only increasing and is partially satisfied by a written treatment plan and complete progress notes. A standardized, written treatment plan with problem definitions, goals, objectives, and interventions in every client's file enhances that uniformity of documentation and offers a means of improving care.

Finally, the social work and human services profession stands to benefit from the use of more precise, measurable objectives to evaluate success in mental health treatment. With the advent of detailed treatment plans, outcome data can be more easily collected to document that interventions are effective in achieving specific goals.

HOW TO DEVELOP A TREATMENT PLAN

The process of developing a treatment plan involves a logical series of steps that build on one another. The foundation of any effective treatment plan is the data gathered in a thorough biopsychosocial assessment. As clients present themselves for treatment, the clinician must sensitively listen in order to understand the issues the client is struggling with—in terms of current stressors, emotional status, social network, physical health, coping skills, interpersonal conflicts, power control, and so on. Assessment data may be gathered from a social history, physical exam, clinical interview, psychological testing inventories, or through the use of genograms. The integration of the data by the clinician or the multidisciplinary treatment team members is critical in understanding the client's issues. Once the assessment is complete, following the six steps listed here will help to ensure the development of a sound treatment plan.

Step One: Problem Selection

This *Social Work and Human Services Treatment Planner* offers 32 problems to select from. Although clients may discuss a variety of issues during the assessment phase, the clinician must ferret out the most significant problems on which to focus the treatment process. Usually a primary problem will surface; secondary problems are more covert and may become evident later. Some problem issues may have to be set aside as insufficiently urgent to warrant treatment at this time. These can be identified as tertiary issues and addressed later. An effective treatment plan can only deal with a few selected problems, or treatment will lose its direction. Thus, priority schedules can and should be used within the treatment planning process.

In choosing which problems to focus on, it is important to note which problems are most acute or disruptive to a client's functioning. The client's motivation to participate in and cooperate with the treatment process depends, to some extent, on the degree to which treatment addresses his or her greatest needs. Obviously, this step will vary depending on the specific treatment modality the clinician chooses to employ. While some therapeutic approaches lend themselves to outlining problems and issues more clearly than others, the clinician is advised to attempt to modify these steps to accommodate the respective approach.

Step Two: Problem Definition

Each individual client uniquely reveals how a problem behaviorally manifests itself in his or her life. Therefore, each problem that is selected for treatment focus must be defined in its relation to the particular client. The symptom pattern should be associated with diagnostic criteria and codes such as those found in the *Diagnostic and Statistical Manual of Mental Disorders, Fourth Edition* (*DSM-IV*) or the *Interna-*

tional Classification of Diseases. The *Social Work and Human Services Treatment Planner,* following the pattern established by *DSM-IV,* offers an array of behaviorally specific problem definition statements. Each of the presenting problems listed in the table of contents has several behavioral symptoms from which to choose. These prewritten definitions may also be used as models in crafting additional definitions.

Step Three: Goal Development

The next step in the treatment planning stage is to set broad goals for the resolution of the target problem. These statements need not to be crafted in measurable terms but, instead, should focus on the global, long-term outcomes of treatment. Although the *Social Work and Human Services Treatment Planner* suggests several possible goal statements for each problem, it is only necessary to select one goal for each treatment plan.

Step Four: Objective Construction

In contrast to long-term goals, objectives must be stated in behaviorally measurable language. It must be clear when the client has achieved the established objectives. Review agencies (e.g., JCAHO), HMOs, and managed care organizations insist that treatment results be measurable. As a result, the objectives presented in this *Social Work and Human Services Treatment Planner* are designed to meet this demand for accountability. Numerous alternatives are presented to allow construction of a variety of treatment plan possibilities for the same presenting problem. The clinician must exercise professional judgment as to which objectives are most appropriate for a given client and how these objectives fit with their particular modality of therapy.

Each objective should be developed as a step toward attaining the broad treatment goal. In essence, objectives can be thought of as a series of steps that, when completed, will result in the achievement of the long-term goal. There should be at least two objectives for each problem, but the clinician may select as many as necessary for goal achievement. Target attainment dates should be listed for each objective. New objectives may be added to the plan as treatment progresses. When all of the necessary objectives have been achieved, the client should have resolved the target problem successfully, or at least be well en route to doing so.

Step Five: Intervention Creation

Interventions are the actions of the clinician designed to help the client complete the objectives. There should be at least one intervention for every objective. If the client does not accomplish the objective after the initial intervention, new interventions should be added to the plan.

Interventions should be selected on the basis of the client's needs and the clinician's full treatment repertoire. This *Social Work and Human Services Treatment Planner* contains interventions from a broad range of therapeutic approaches, including cognitive, dynamic, behavioral, pharmacological, systems-oriented, experiential/expressive, and solution-focused brief therapy. It should be kept in mind, however, that not all modalities of treatment adhere to treatment planning in the same way. Depending on the specific modality of treatment, the mere concept of a treatment plan at all may be incongruous with the basic tenet of the approach. Consequently, it is left to the treating clinician to chose a treatment modality that will lend itself to effective treatment planning.

Step Six: Diagnosis Determination

The determination of an appropriate diagnosis is based on an evaluation of the client's complete clinical presentation. The clinician must compare the behavioral, cognitive, emotional, and interpersonal symptoms that the client presents to the criteria for diagnosis of a mental illness as described in *DSM-IV*. Careful assessment of behavioral indicators facilitate a more accurate diagnosis and more effective treatment planning.

HOW TO USE THIS PLANNER

Acquiring skill in composing effective treatment plans can be a tedious and difficult process for many clinicians. The *Social Work and Human Services Treatment Planner* was developed as a tool to aid clinicians in quickly writing treatment plans that are clear, specific, and customized to the particular needs of each client. Treatment plans should be developed by moving, in turn, through each of the following steps:

1. Choose one presenting problem with the client that you have identified in the assessment process. Locate the corresponding page number for that problem in the *Social Work and Human Services Treatment Planner*'s table of contents.
2. Select two or three of the listed behavioral definitions and record them in the appropriate section on the treatment plan form.
3. Select a single long-term goal, and record it in the Goals section of the treatment plan form.

4. Review the listed objectives for this problem and select the ones clinically indicated for the client. Remember, it is recommended that at least two objectives be selected for each problem. Add a target date or the number of sessions allocated for the attainment of each objective.

5. Choose relevant interventions. The numbers of the interventions most salient to each objective are listed in parentheses following the objective statement. Feel free to choose other interventions from the list, or to add new interventions as needed in the space provided.

6. *DSM-IV* diagnoses that are commonly associated with the problem are listed at the end of each chapter. These diagnoses are meant to be suggestions for clinical consideration. Select a diagnosis listed or assign a more appropriate choice from the *DSM-IV.*

Note: To accommodate those practitioners who tend to plan treatment in terms of diagnostic labels rather than presenting problems, the appendix lists all of the *DSM-IV* diagnoses that are included in the Planner, cross-referenced to the problems related to each diagnosis.

Following these steps will facilitate the development of complete, customized treatment plans ready for immediate implementation and presentation to the clients. The final plan should resemble the format of the sample plan presented at the end of this introduction.

ELECTRONIC TREATMENT PLANNING

As paperwork mounts, more and more clinicians are turning to computerized record keeping. The presenting problems, goals, objectives, interventions, and diagnoses in the *Social Work and Human Services Treatment Planner* are available in electronic form as an add-on upgrade module to the popular software Thera*Scribe®*, the latest version of the popular treatment planning and patient record-keeping software. For more information on Thera*Scribe®* or the social work and human services add-on module, call John Wiley & Sons at 1-800-379-4539, or mail in the information request coupon at the back of this book.

A WORD OF CAUTION

Whether using the print Planner or the electronic version, it is critical to remember that effective treatment planning requires that each plan be tailored to the specific client's problems and needs. Treatment plans should not be mass-produced, even if clients have similar problems. Each client's strengths and weaknesses, unique stressors, social network, individual circumstances, and interactional patterns must be considered in developing a treatment strategy. The clinically derived statements in this Planner can be combined in thousands of permutations to develop detailed treatment plans. In addition, readers are encouraged to add their own definitions, goals, objectives, and interventions to the existing samples, particularly as they pertain to their respective mode of treatment. Clinicians are also urged to proceed with treatment planning in a manner that ensures the utmost confidentiality.

SAMPLE TREATMENT PLAN

PROBLEM: RAPE VICTIM

Behavioral   Self-report of sexual assault victimization.
Definitions: Evidence of rape: bruises; lacerations; broken bones; red, swollen, or torn genitalia; and/or open sores.
Intrusive, distressing thoughts, flashbacks, or images that recall the rape.
Fearful isolation and withdrawal in an attempt to protect self from anticipated future victimization.
Depressed affect, low energy, sleep disturbance, and tearful spells.

Goals: Reduce the negative impact that the rape has had on many aspects of life and return to pretrauma level of functioning.
Recall the rape without becoming overwhelmed with negative emotions.

Short-Term Objectives	Therapeutic Interventions
1. Cooperate with a referral to a physician for a medical status assessment.	1. Refer the client to a physician to rule out any medical conditions that are in need of immediate treatment.
	2. Refer the client to a rape crisis team for completion of a medically administered rape kit for evidentiary purposes.
2. Describe the rape in as much detail as possible.	1. Build rapport with the client through consistent eye contact, unconditional positive regard, warm acceptance, soft voice, conversation about non-threatening topics, and expressions of reassurance regarding the client's safety.
	2. Slowly and gently explore the details of the rape without pressing the client beyond his/her ability to trust or to cope with emotions associated with the assault.

3. Identify the feelings experienced at the time of the rape.	1. Encourage and support the client in verbally expressing and clarifying his/her feelings at the time of the rape.
4. Describe any fears regarding the perpetrator seeking revenge for being reported.	1. Assess the client's safety from retaliation by the perpetrator of the rape; facilitate the client's obtaining a place of safety. 2. Facilitate and encourage the client's making contact with legal authorities to obtain protection from further threat of assault and to report the crime.
5. Verbalize agreement that the responsibility for the rape falls on the perpetrator, not on self.	1. Confront the client for excusing the perpetrator and reinforce all statements that place clear responsibility on the perpetrator of the rape. 2. Provide a more reality-based view of the circumstances of the rape when the client tends to take on blame for the rape or excuse the perpetrator's actions.
6. Accept referral to a support group for rape survivors.	1. Refer the client to a support group for rape survivors.

Diagnosis: 308.3   Acute Stress Disorder

Note: The numbers in parentheses accompanying the short-term objectives in each chapter correspond to the list of suggested therapeutic interventions in that chapter. Each objective has specific interventions that have been designed to assist the client in attaining that objective. Clinical judgment should determine the exact intervention to be used, including any outside of those suggested.

ALCOHOL ABUSE/DEPENDENCE

BEHAVIORAL DEFINITIONS

1. Consistent use of alcohol until high, intoxicated, or passed out.
2. Inability to stop or cut down use of alcohol once started, despite the verbalized desire to do so and the negative consequences continued use brings.
3. Blood work that reflects the results of a pattern of heavy alcohol use—for example, elevated liver enzymes.
4. Denial that alcohol use is a problem despite direct feedback from spouse, relatives, friends, and employers that the use of alcohol is negatively affecting them and others.
5. Occurrence of amnesiac blackouts when abusing alcohol.
6. Continued alcohol use despite experiencing persistent or recurring physical, legal, vocational, social, or relationship problems that are directly caused by the use of alcohol.
7. Increased tolerance for alcohol as there is the need to use more to become intoxicated or to attain the desired effect.
8. Physical symptoms—that is, shaking, seizures, nausea, headaches, sweating, anxiety, insomnia, and/or depression—when withdrawing from alcohol.
9. Suspension of important social, recreational, or occupational activities because they interfere with consuming alcohol.
10. Large time investment in activities to obtain alcohol, to use it, or to recover from its effects.
11. Consumption of alcohol in greater amounts and for longer periods than intended.
12. Continued use of alcohol after being told by a physician that it is causing health problems.
13. Expression of worry by loved ones that the client is drinking excessively.
14. Aggressive, abusive, or violent behavior when drinking alcohol.
15. Neglect of family obligations due to alcohol abuse.

16. Neglect of responsibilities at work or at school because of drinking alcohol.
17. Expression of fear of the client by loved ones when he/she is drinking excessively.
18. Poor health, low self-esteem, unemployment, broken relationships, and financial stress as a result of chronic alcohol dependence.
19. Homelessness, depression, and social isolation as a result of chronic alcohol dependence.

—. _____

_____

—. _____

_____

—. _____

_____

LONG-TERM GOALS

1. Accept chemical dependence and begin to actively participate in a recovery program.
2. Withdraw from alcohol, stabilize physically and emotionally, and then establish a supportive recovery plan.
3. Improve quality of life by maintaining an ongoing abstinence from all mood-altering chemicals.
4. Reduce drinking to a level at which school or work are not negatively impacted.
5. Reduce drinking to a level at which loved ones are not negatively impacted.
6. Maintain alcohol consumption at an acceptable level.

—. _____

_____

—. _____

_____

—. _____

_____

SHORT-TERM OBJECTIVES

1. Describe the details regarding the nature, extent, and frequency of alcohol consumption. (1)
2. Participate in medical examination to assess the consequences of alcohol abuse. (2)
3. Obtain ongoing recommended medical care. (3, 4)
4. Obtain information regarding negative nutritional consequences of chronic alcohol abuse and current nutritional rehabilitation needs. (5)
5. Describe the negative consequences of alcohol abuse to self and loved ones. (1, 6, 7)
6. Verbalize an increased understanding of the physical and psychological effects of alcohol abuse. (8, 9)
7. Accept referral for further assessment of alcohol abuse. (10)
8. Participate in alcohol counseling and treatment. (11)
9. Attend Alcoholics Anonymous (AA) meetings on a frequent and consistent basis. (12, 13)
10. List sources of stress and pressure that provide the impetus for escape into alcohol abuse. (14)

THERAPEUTIC INTERVENTIONS

1. Convey a warm, nonjudgmental approach when eliciting information from the client regarding his/her history of alcohol abuse.
2. Refer the client to a physician for examination of the medical consequences of the alcohol abuse.
3. Obtain written confidentiality release from the client to allow for contract with the evaluating professional to share information regarding the abuse and obtain the results and recommendations of the evaluation.
4. Facilitate and monitor the client's access to more medical services as recommended by the examining physician.
5. Refer the client for a nutritional assessment, education as to the effects of alcohol abuse on nutrition, and recommendations regarding nutritional rehabilitation.
6. Assist the client in listing the negative consequences of alcohol abuse (e.g., vocational, legal, familial, medical, social, and financial).
7. Confront the client when he/she minimizes his/her alcohol abuse or its negative impact.

11. Cooperate with a referral to resources for stress reduction. (15, 16)

12. Family members verbalize an increased understanding of alcohol abuse and treatment. (9, 17)

13. Family members accept a referral to support group. (18)

14. Utilize the services of a shelter for the homeless. (19)

15. Obtain vocational rehabilitation services as a step toward reemployment. (20)

16. Demonstrate compliance with the treatment plan. (21, 22, 23)

—. _____
_____

—. _____
_____

—. _____
_____

8. Provide the client with specific information on the physical and psychological effects of alcohol abuse.

9. Refer the client and family to literature that explains the symptoms, consequences, and treatment of alcohol dependence (e.g., *I'll Quit Tomorrow* [Johnson] or *Many Roads, One Journey* [Kasl-Davis]).

10. Refer the client for a psychological evaluation for assessment of alcohol abuse and any related cognitive, emotional, and behavioral disorders.

11. Coordinate the client's obtaining ongoing treatment for alcohol dependence and psychological problems resulting from alcohol abuse; refer the client to an appropriate counseling provider.

12. Refer the client to Alcoholics Anonymous (AA); contact an AA member to accompany the client to a first-step meeting, if necessary.

13. Process the client's experience at AA and reinforce consistent attendance and participation.

14. Assist the client in identifying the sources of pain or stress that foster escape into alcohol abuse.

15. Refer the client to classes that teach stress management techniques.

16. Refer the client to a counseling resource for learning

stress-coping and stress-reduction approaches.

17. Provide family members with education regarding alcohol-abuse symptoms, prognosis, and treatment options.

18. Link family members to self-help groups in the community (e.g., Alanon, Alateen, and Tough Love).

19. Facilitate the client's admission to a facility or shelter for the homeless.

20. Refer the client to vocational rehabilitation counseling as a precursor to becoming employed.

21. Monitor the client's follow-through on linking with service providers.

22. Reinforce the importance of following through with linkages and treatment.

23. Monitor compliance by the client and family with the treatment plan.

__. _____
   _____

__. _____
   _____

__. _____
   _____

DIAGNOSTIC SUGGESTIONS

Axis I: 303.90 Alcohol Dependence
305.00 Alcohol Abuse
304.80 Polysubstance Dependence

	312.34	Intermittent Explosive Disorder
	309.81	Posttraumatic Stress Disorder
	_____	_____
	_____	_____
Axis II:	301.7	Antisocial Personality Disorder
	V71.09	No Diagnosis on Axis II
	799.9	Diagnosis Deferred on Axis II
	_____	_____
	_____	_____

ASSAULTIVE BEHAVIOR

BEHAVIORAL DEFINITIONS

1. Episodes of loss of control of aggressive impulses out of proportion to the situation and resulting in assaultive acts and/or destruction of property.
2. Use of verbally abusive language intended to berate, intimidate, or hurt others.
3. Use of minimization, denial, and projection of responsibility in describing physical abuse of others.
4. Failure to conform with social norms with respect to the law, as shown by repeated performance of antisocial acts that may or may not have resulted in arrests.
5. Refusal to follow rules, with the attitude that they apply only to others.
6. History of criminal activity leading to numerous arrests and current court involvement.
7. Abuse of alcohol and/or drugs.

—. _____
_____

—. _____
_____

—. _____
_____

LONG-TERM GOALS

1. Terminate physically and verbally aggressive acts.
2. Develop and demonstrate a healthy sense of respect for social norms, the rights of others, and the need for honesty.

3. Accept responsibility for own actions, including apologizing for hurts and not blaming others.
4. Come to an understanding and acceptance of the need for limits, rules, and boundaries on behavior.
5. Understand how substance abuse has contributed to assaultive behavior and accept the need for recovery.
6. Learn to stop, think, listen, and plan before acting.

—. _____
_____
_____

—. _____
_____
_____

—. _____
_____

SHORT-TERM OBJECTIVES

1. Identify the physically and verbally aggressive acts that have been exhibited over the past year. (1)

2. List the reasons or rewards that have led to a pattern of aggressive behavior. (2)

3. List the negative consequences that accrue to self and others as a result of aggressive behaviors. (3, 4)

4. Admit to aggressive behavior that has trampled on the law and/or the rights and feelings of others. (1, 5)

5. Identify the thoughts and feelings that have triggered the aggressive behavior. (6)

6. List alternative coping responses to triggers to abusive behavior. (7)

THERAPEUTIC INTERVENTIONS

1. Explore and document instances of the client's aggressive behavior.

2. Help the client list the positive results he/she gets from aggressive actions and process the list.

3. Help the client list the negative consequences that have occurred because of his/her aggression.

4. Help the client make a connection between aggression and the negative outcomes experienced.

5. Confront the client's denial of responsibility for his/her aggressive behavior and the negative consequences.

6. Explore the client's thoughts and feelings that trigger his/her aggressive behavior.

7. Verbalize an understanding of the benefits for self and others of living within the laws and rules of society. (8, 9, 10)

8. List relationships that have been broken or damaged because of physical and verbal aggression. (11, 12)

9. List those who deserve an apology for hurtful behaviors. (11, 12, 13, 14)

10. Indicate steps that will be taken to make amends for hurt caused to others. (14, 15)

11. Describe the amount, frequency, and history of substance abuse. (16)

12. Identify the negative consequences of alcohol and/or drug abuse. (17, 18)

13. Cooperate with an alcohol and/or drug evaluation. (19)

14. Terminate substance abuse through participation in a recovery program. (20)

15. Accept a referral to individual counseling focused on terminating aggressive behavior. (21)

16. Consistently attend and participate in group therapy treatment. (22)

17. Family participates in family therapy. (23)

18. Fulfill the court requirements pertaining to sentencing for assault. (24, 25)

7. Teach the client cognitive and behavioral coping mechanisms for thoughts and feelings that have historically triggered physical abuse (e.g., time-out, deep breathing, physical exercise, escalation avoidance procedure, etc.).

8. Teach the client that the basis for social trust is lawfulness, which precludes anarchy in society.

9. Solicit a commitment to live a prosocial, law-abiding lifestyle.

10. Emphasize the reality of negative consequences for the client if continued lawlessness is practiced.

11. Review relationships that have been broken or damaged due to the client's antisocial attitudes and behaviors.

12. Confront the client's lack of sensitivity to the needs and feelings of others.

13. Assist the client in listing individuals who deserve amends for his/her hurtful behavior.

14. Teach the value of apologizing for hurt caused as a means of accepting responsibility for behavior.

15. Encourage a commitment by the client to take specific steps that will make amends for his/her actions.

16. Explore with the client his/her use of mood-altering substances.

___. _____
_____
___. _____
_____
___. _____
_____

17. Assist the client in listing the negative consequences substance abuse has had on his/her life.

18. Help the client make the connection between his/her substance abuse and aggression.

19. Evaluate the client for chemical dependence or refer the client to an alcohol and drug counselor for evaluation.

20. Refer the client for chemical dependence treatment and to AA.

21. Facilitate a referral to individual counseling for the client.

22. Refer the client to group treatment for aggressive behavior.

23. Refer the family for family therapy.

24. Guide and monitor the client's cooperation with and fulfillment of the sentencing of the court resulting from arrest for assault.

25. Facilitate the family's or spouse's obtaining a court order restraining the client from close physical proximity to family members.

___. _____
_____
___. _____
_____
___. _____
_____

DIAGNOSTIC SUGGESTIONS

Axis I: 312.34   Intermittent Explosive Disorder
                V71.01   Adult Antisocial Behavior
                309.3   Adjustment Disorder With Disturbance of
                            Conduct
                312.8   Conduct Disorder
                303.90   Alcohol Dependence

                _____   _____

                _____   _____

Axis II: 301.7   Antisocial Personality Disorder
                301.83   Borderline Personality Disorder
                V71.09   No Diagnosis on Axis II
                799.9   Diagnosis Deferred on Axis II

                _____   _____

                _____   _____

ASSAULT VICTIM

BEHAVIORAL DEFINITIONS

1. Self-report of verbal and physical assault.
2. Reports by family, friends, neighbors, or police that client was a victim of verbal and physical assault.
3. Evidence of physical assault: bruises, broken bones, and/or lacerations.
4. Intrusive, distressing thoughts, flashbacks, or images that recall the assault.
5. Inability to recall some aspects of the assault.
6. Physiological reactivity and intense distress when exposed to cues that symbolize the assault.
7. Avoidance of activity, people, or places associated with the assault.
8. Depressed affect, low energy, sleep disturbances, and tearful spells.
9. Alcohol and/or drug abuse.

__. _____

_____

__. _____

_____

__. _____

_____

LONG-TERM GOALS

1. Reduce the negative impact that the assault has had on many aspects of life and return to pretrauma level of functioning.
2. Develop and implement effective coping skills in order to carry out normal responsibilities and participate constructively in relationships.

3. Recall the assault without becoming overwhelmed with negative emotions.
4. Terminate destructive behaviors and implement behaviors that promote healing, acceptance of assault, and responsible living.

—. _____

_____

—. _____

_____

—. _____

_____

SHORT-TERM OBJECTIVES

1. Cooperate with a referral to a physician for a medical assessment. (1)
2. Describe the assault in as much detail as possible. (2, 3)
3. Express the feelings that were experienced at the time of the assault. (4)
4. Describe any fears regarding the perpetrator seeking revenge for being reported. (5)
5. Agree to and then make contact with legal authorities to seek protection for self. (6, 7, 8)
6. Cooperate with legal authorities under the guidance of an attorney. (7)
7. Verbalize an understanding of the legal process of police investigation and court proceedings. (8)
8. Verbalize that the responsibility for the assault be-

THERAPEUTIC INTERVENTIONS

1. Refer the client to a physician to rule out any medical conditions that are in need of immediate treatment.
2. Built rapport with the client through consistent eye contact, unconditional positive regard, warm acceptance, soft voice, conversation about nonthreatening topics, and expressions of reassurance regarding the client's safety.
3. Slowly and gently explore the details of the assault without pressing the client beyond his/her ability to trust or cope with the emotional impact of the incident.
4. Explore the client's emotional reaction at the time of the assault.
5. Assess the client's safety from retaliation by the perpetrator of the assault; facilitate the client's finding a place of safety.

longs to the perpetrator, not self. (9, 10)

9. Accept a referral for individual counseling. (11)

10. Describe the amount, history, and frequency of substance abuse used to cope with trauma. (12)

11. Identify the negative consequences of substance abuse as a coping behavior. (13)

12. Accept a referral for drug and/or alcohol evaluation and treatment. (14)

13. Accept a referral to a support group for assault victims. (15)

14. Identify sources of support among family and friends. (16)

15. Increase the level of trust of others, as shown by more socialization. (17, 18)

16. Verbalize hopeful and positive statements regarding the future. (19, 20)

—. _____

_____

—. _____

_____

—. _____

_____

6. Encourage the client to make contact with legal authorities to obtain protection from further assault.

7. Encourage and empower the client to assert his/her right to protection from the law by testifying against the perpetrator; refer him/her to a victim advocacy program.

8. Explain to the client the legal process that will ensue due to the assault.

9. Confront the client for excusing the perpetrator and reinforce all statements that place clear responsibility on the perpetrator of the assault.

10. Provide a more reality-based view of circumstances of the assault as the client tends to take on blame for the assault or excuse the perpetrator's actions.

11. Refer the client to individual counseling to assist him/her in overcoming the traumatic effects of the assault.

12. Gather data from the client regarding the amount, frequency, and history of his/her substance abuse as a means of coping with the feelings of anger and anxiety related to the assault.

13. Teach the client the negative consequences of abusing substances as a means of coping with fear, anger,

and anxiety (e.g., exacerbation of negative emotions; precipitation of chemical dependence; and precipitation of relational, vocational, and legal problems).

14. Refer the client to drug and/or alcohol counseling for an evaluation of substance abuse or dependence.

15. Refer the client to a support group for assault victims.

16. Assist the client in identifying people that he/she can turn to for understanding and support.

17. Teach the client the share-check method of building trust (i.e., sharing only a little of self and then checking to be sure that the shared data is treated respectfully, kindly, and confidentially; as proof of trustworthiness is verified, share more freely).

18. Encourage and reinforce the client's reaching out for social and emotional support rather than withdrawing into isolation.

19. Reinforce positive, reality-based messages that enhance self-confidence and increase adaptive action.

20. Assist the client in listing positive goals for his/her future rather than becoming fixated on the trauma of the past.

__.__ _____
       _____
       _____

__.__ _____
       _____
       _____

__.__ _____
       _____

DIAGNOSTIC SUGGESTIONS

Axis I:	309.81	Posttraumatic Stress Disorder
	309.xx	Adjustment Disorder
	308.3	Acute Stress Disorder
	296.xx	Major Depressive Disorder
	300.00	Anxiety Disorder NOS
	_____	_____
	_____	_____
Axis II:	V71.09	No Diagnosis on Axis II
	799.9	Diagnosis Deferred on Axis II
	_____	_____
	_____	_____

CHILD PHYSICAL/VERBAL ABUSE

BEHAVIORAL DEFINITIONS

1. Shoving, pushing, or scratching a child.
2. Pinching or biting a child.
3. Hitting, punching, or kicking a child.
4. Choking or strangling a child.
5. Violently shaking a child.
6. Using weapons or instruments to hurt a child.
7. Belittling or ridiculing a child in the family.
8. Insulting or shaming a child in front of others.
9. Yelling at or threatening a child.
10. Threatening another family member in front of a child.
11. Child observing physical violence between adults in a family.
12. Child observing verbal abuse between adults in a family.

—. _____

_____

—. _____

_____

—. _____

_____

LONG-TERM GOALS

1. Eliminate physical abuse of the child.
2. Develop a safe physical environment for the child or place him/her in one.
3. Eliminate verbal abuse of the child.
4. Develop an adequate psychosocial environment for the child's development.

5. Reduce stress in the parental environment.
6. Increase marital compatibility and communication.
7. Develop adequate parenting skills.
8. Develop adequate negotiation skills.

—. _____

   _____

—. _____

   _____

—. _____

   _____

SHORT-TERM OBJECTIVES

1. Describe conditions of environment, eating habits, treatment, and supervision by caregivers. (1, 2)

2. Verbalize an understanding of the need to be moved to a safer environment. (1, 3, 4)

3. Accept placement in the home of a relative. (1, 5)

4. Accept placement in a temporary foster home. (6, 7, 8)

5. Accept placement in a residential facility. (6, 9, 10)

6. Verbalize acceptance of the adults who will serve as caregivers. (3, 11)

7. Parents express their feelings about their child being removed from their home. (12)

8. Parents verbalize an understanding of the criteria that must be met before the family can be reunited. (12, 13)

THERAPEUTIC INTERVENTIONS

1. Ascertain, through physical inspection of the premises and individual interviews with caregivers, neighbors, and the child or children, whether caregivers are able to provide a physically and emotionally safe environment for the child.

2. If it is determined that the child needs to be removed for his/her physical and emotional safety, move to terminate parental rights.

3. Meet with the child and explain the concern for his/her safety and his/her need for supervision, nurturance, and love, leading to the need for placement in a supportive environment.

4. Reassure the child of your interest in his/her safety and need for love; promise continued attempts to rectify the problems of the

9. Verbalize an acceptance of the schedule for continued contact with parents. (14)

10. Parents demonstrate reduced frequency and intensity of yelling, scolding, swearing, name-calling, and belittling directed at the children. (15, 16)

11. Parents verbalize reasonable expectations of the child commensurate with the child's level of psychosocial development. (17)

12. Parents implement relaxation strategies to cope with stress. (18)

13. Parents identify and implement pleasurable activities that reduce stress. (19)

14. Parents attend counseling to learn stress-reduction skills. (20, 21, 22)

15. Parents attend classes to learn effective parenting skills. (23)

16. Report adequate supervision, nurturant care, and absence of physical or verbal abuse. (24, 25)

—. _____
   _____

—. _____
   _____

—. _____
   _____

parental home and reunite the family.

5. Explore whether there are any other family members able to provide a safe, nurturing environment for the child or children on a temporary basis.

6. Make contact with the probate court to arrange for temporary court custody of the child.

7. Make arrangements to place the child in a temporary foster home.

8. Facilitate the transfer of the child to the foster home.

9. Arrange for the child's evaluation and admission at a residential treatment facility.

10. Facilitate the child's transfer to the residential facility.

11. Conduct a joint session with the child and new caregiver to introduce each to the other and give the child an opportunity to express his/her feelings and ask questions.

12. Meet with the neglectful or abusive parents to explain the need for the removal of the child from the home; reassure them regarding the process of treatment for them and regarding the return of the child to the home, contingent on their making environmental and behavioral changes.

13. Develop markers (e.g., complete a parenting class, pursue marital counseling, and demonstrate regular attendance at family therapy sessions and consistent responsibility in supervised visitation) that parents must satisfy before reunification of the family is possible.

14. Schedule visits between child and parents while child is temporarily removed from parents' custody.

15. Monitor and supervise parental visits to teach and reinforce calm, respectful child-management skills.

16. Alert the parents to focus on reducing negative physical (e.g., hitting, grabbing, spanking, and slapping) and verbal (e.g., yelling, swearing, name-calling, and scolding) contact, as well as threats, substituting positive parental communication skills instead.

17. Teach the parents reasonable expectations for each level of a child's psychosocial development.

18. Enroll the parents in classes that teach relaxation training (e.g., yoga and meditation).

19. Assist the parents in identifying pleasurable activities (e.g., hobbies, sports, music, dancing, hiking, and bike riding) that would enrich

their lives as well as reduce stress; structure times for implementation of these activities.

20. Assist the parents in identifying stressors (e.g., financial pressures, substance abuse, depression, social isolation, and extended family conflict) that increase frustration and exacerbate the likelihood of venting anger at the children.

21. Refer the parents for counseling to learn coping skills for stress.

22. Facilitate and monitor the parents' follow-through on obtaining counseling.

23. Refer the parents to a parenting-skills group.

24. Schedule regular contact with the child for interviews and assessment regarding the caregivers' provision of safe, nurturant, affirming care.

25. Maintain contact with the court to keep it informed of the child's welfare and the parents' progress in meeting the criteria for uniting the family.

__. _____

_____

__. _____

_____

__. _____

_____

DIAGNOSTIC SUGGESTIONS:

Axis I:	309.24	Adjustment Disorder With Anxiety
	309.0	Adjustment Disorder With Depressed Mood
	312.34	Intermittent Explosive Disorder
	995.5	Physical Abuse of Child (Victim)
	_____	_____
	_____	_____
Axis II:	301.82	Avoidant Personality Disorder
	301.7	Antisocial Personality Disorder
	_____	_____
	_____	_____

DRUG ABUSE/DEPENDENCE

BEHAVIORAL DEFINITIONS

1. Maladaptive pattern of substance use manifested by increased tolerance and withdrawal.
2. Inability to stop or cut down use of mood-altering drug despite the verbalized desire to do so and the negative consequences of continued use.
3. Denial that chemical dependence is a problem despite feedback from significant others that the substance use is negatively affecting them.
4. Continued substance use despite persistent physical, legal, financial, vocational, social, or relationship problems that are directly caused by the substance use.
5. Increased drug tolerance as increased substance use is required to become intoxicated or to recall the desired effect.
6. Physical withdrawal symptoms (shaking, seizures, nausea, headaches, sweating, anxiety, insomnia, and/or depression) when going without the substance for any length of time.
7. Arrests for substance abuse-related offenses (e.g., driving under the influence, minor in possession, assault, possession or delivery of a controlled substance, and shoplifting).
8. Suspension of important social, recreational, or occupational activities because they interfere with using.
9. Large time investment in activities to obtain the substance, use it, or recover from its effects.
10. Inhalation or sniffing of substances such as glue and solvents.
11. Use of illegal drugs in the presence of children.
12. Ingestion of medicine in larger doses than prescribed.
13. Abuse of nonprescription drugs.
14. Aggressive or abusive behavior toward others when under the influence of the drug.

15. Drug use by a family member creating problems at work or school.
16. Neglect of obligations within the family when using drugs.

___. _____

_____

___. _____

_____

_____

___. _____

_____

LONG-TERM GOALS

1. Accept powerlessness over and inability to manage mood-altering substances and participate in a recovery-based program.
2. Improve quality of life by maintaining abstinence from all mood-altering chemicals.
3. Withdraw from mood-altering substance, stabilize physically and emotionally, and then establish a supportive recovery plan.
4. Eliminate the misuse of prescribed or over-the-counter drugs and medications.
5. Family members reside in a safe physical environment during the client's recovery period.
6. Eliminate work, school, or family problems precipitated by drug abuse.
7. Eliminate aggressive, violent, or abusive behavior due to drug abuse.
8. Increase fulfillment of duties or obligations at home, work, and/or school.

___. _____

_____

___. _____

_____

___. _____

_____

SHORT-TERM OBJECTIVES

1. Describe the amount, frequency, and history of substance abuse. (1)
2. Client and family members recognize physical and behavioral signs of drug abuse (e.g., abusive verbal or physical behavior, incoherence, memory loss, uncharacteristic behavior, and personality changes). (2)
3. Describe the home environment and allow an inspection of the premises. (3)
4. Identify the negative consequences of drug and/or alcohol abuse. (4)
5. Family members recognize that the client's drug abuse is the cause of family, school, or work problems. (2, 5, 6)
6. Family members and the client verbalize an understanding of drug abuse treatment and each of their roles in treatment. (7, 8)
7. Client and family members consent to participate in a treatment program to reduce the client's drug abuse. (9, 10)
8. Describe the currently prescribed medications and their effectiveness. (11, 12)
9. Participate in a medical evaluation of the effectiveness of the prescribed medications. (13, 14, 15)

THERAPEUTIC INTERVENTIONS

1. Gather a complete drug and alcohol history including amount and pattern of use, signs and symptoms of use, and negative life consequences (social, legal, familial, and vocational).
2. Provide information to the client and family members regarding the signs of drug abuse (e.g., abusive or aggressive behavior during drug use episodes; behavioral and personality changes that are evident with drug abuse).
3. Ascertain, through physical inspection of the home and individual interviews with caregivers, neighbors, and family members, whether the physical and emotional environment is safe for family members.
4. Ask the client to make a list of the ways substance abuse has negatively impacted his/her life and process it with the therapist.
5. Assist the family in identifying problems in the home, school, or workplace that are precipitated by a client's or family member's drug use (e.g., child or spouse abuse or neglect, absenteeism from school or work, loss of a job, or arrest for driving while under the influence).

10. Family members describe their level of concern for their safety and/or for getting their basic needs met. (3, 16)

11. Family members or spouse move to a safe and supportive environment. (17)

12. Family members obtain supportive services. (18, 19, 21)

13. Family members and the client participate in Narcotics Anonymous (NA) meetings. (20)

14. Report absence of drug abuse in home, school, or work environments. (10, 15, 21)

—. _____
   _____

—. _____
   _____

—. _____
   _____

6. Guide the client and family members in identifying the consequences to each member when drugs are abused.

7. Provide the client and family members information regarding the diagnoses, treatment, and prognosis for drug abuse.

8. Assist the family in identifying individual roles and responsibilities in the treatment of drug abuse.

9. Assess the level of care (e.g., inpatient, outpatient, or intensive outpatient) necessary to most effectively treat the client's drug dependence, considering the client's chronicity of drug use, degree of physiological dependence, available support system, and previous treatment.

10. Refer the client and family members to the appropriate level of care (e.g., inpatient, outpatient, or intensive outpatient) for the client's drug abuse problem.

11. Review the client's prescribed medications and schedules with the client and family members.

12. Explore the client's evaluation of the effectiveness of the currently prescribed medication regimen (e.g., effectiveness in reducing pain or symptoms).

13. If it is determined that the current medication regimen

is ineffective, refer the client for a medical consultation and evaluation.

14. Follow up with the client to determine his/her assessment of the medical consultation.

15. Urge the client to adhere strictly to prescribed dosages of medication and to report honestly to the physician regarding the effectiveness of the medication.

16. Assess the care, nurturance, and safety of all family members, especially minors, while in the company of the drug-abusing family member.

17. If it is determined that the child or family member needs to be removed for his/her physical and emotional safety, refer to or place in an appropriate environment (e.g., temporary foster home, family shelter, or women's safe house).

18. Refer the family to appropriate social services (e.g., protective services, family counseling, and financial relief services) to assist them in coping with the hardships resulting from the consequences of drug abuse in the family and/or the necessary relocation for safety and nurturance.

19. Facilitate and monitor the client's and family members' follow-through on ac-

quiring appropriate counseling or services.

20. Refer the client to Narcotics Anonymous (NA) and the family members to Alanon.

21. Schedule regular contact with the family members to review progress.

—. _____
_____

—. _____
_____

—. _____
_____

DIAGNOSTIC SUGGESTIONS

Axis I:	304.30	Cannabis Dependence
	305.20	Cannabis Abuse
	304.20	Cocaine Dependence
	305.60	Cocaine Abuse
	304.80	Polysubstance Dependence
	V71.01	Adult Antisocial Behavior
	312.34	Intermittent Explosive Disorder
	309.81	Posttraumatic Stress Disorder
	304.10	Sedative, Hypnotic, or Anxiolytic Dependence
	_____	_____
	_____	_____
Axis II:	301.7	Antisocial Personality Disorder
	_____	_____
	_____	_____

EMPLOYMENT CONFLICTS

BEHAVIORAL DEFINITIONS

1. Has been unemployed for most of the past 5 years.
2. Does not get along well with coworkers.
3. Is unhappy with job (e.g., finds it boring, inadequate, or hazardous).
4. Has difficulty keeping a job.
5. Is treated unfairly by employer, supervisor, or coworker.
6. Works at a job below his/her ability or training.
7. Is not respected by coworkers.
8. Is unable to work due to physical problems.
9. Is unable to work due to emotional problems.
10. Has difficulty arranging for child care during work hours.
11. Suffers verbal, emotional, or physical abuse at work.
12. Is frequently reprimanded or penalized for being absent or late for work, inadequate performance, or negative attitude.

___. _____
_____
___. _____
_____
___. _____
_____

LONG-TERM GOALS

1. Maintain steady employment.
2. Obtain services to ensure financial assistance, emotional support, medical care, rehabilitation assistance, and so on if physically or emotionally unable to work.

3. Achieve reasonable satisfaction with job or position, employer, and coworkers.
4. Eliminate unfair treatment (discrimination, harassment, and verbal, physical, or emotional abuse) by employer or supervisor and/or coworkers.
5. Obtain employment reflective of interests and abilities.
6. Obtain child/elder/spousal care during times of employment.

—. _____
  _____
  _____

—. _____
  _____
  _____

—. _____
  _____

SHORT-TERM OBJECTIVES

1. Express concern regarding current employment situation. (1, 2)
2. Identify sources of dissatisfaction and clarify the problems. (3, 4, 5)
3. Verbalize a recognition of the interpersonal and familial stressors that contribute to the employment conflict situation. (6)
4. Identify the options for counseling to learn stress-coping skills. (7)
5. Decide on appropriate options for employment problem resolution and implement the options. (7, 8)
6. Outline the steps and skills necessary for job seeking. (9, 10)
7. Express the need for assistance with family responsi-

THERAPEUTIC INTERVENTIONS

1. Explore the client's current employment situation (e.g., what he/she likes or dislikes, working conditions, cause of unemployment, and assessment of abilities).
2. Explore the client's history of unemployment and the factors contributing to it.
3. Ascertain whether the client has the necessary work skills, abilities, and on-the-job social skills for employment.
4. Assist the client in analyzing the current source of job dissatisfaction (e.g., lack of necessary work skills, poor attitude, lack of social skills, or pressures at home due to job situation).
5. Teach the client reasonable expectations for his/her job situation.

bilities that interfere with employment. (11)

8. Identify options for assistance with family responsibilities. (12)

9. Select and implement an option for assistance with family care responsibilities. (13)

10. Verbalize the need for services to ensure financial security, emotional support, medical care, and rehabilitation assistance during periods of employment conflict. (14, 15)

11. Identify options for government or privately supported family assistance services. (16)

12. Select and implement an option for family assistance services. (16, 17)

13. Report improved satisfaction with the job, steady employment, acquisition of services, and so on. (18, 19, 20)

__. _____
_____

__. _____
_____

__. _____
_____

6. Assist the client in identifying stressors (interpersonal or at home) that increase his/her frustration and exacerbate the job situation.

7. Review with the client counseling options that offer training in stress-coping skills, assertiveness, anger control, vocational rehabilitation, and job-skills.

8. Facilitate and monitor the client's follow-through on counseling.

9. Ascertain whether the client has appropriate job-seeking skills.

10. Provide training in job-seeking skills (see *Job Club Counselor's Manual* [Azrin and Besalel]).

11. Explore the client's need for assistance with family responsibilities (e.g., child care, elder care, or respite care) that interfere with employment.

12. Assist the client in identifying options for assistance with family responsibilities, day care, respite care, and so on.

13. Facilitate and reinforce the client's obtaining assistance with family responsibilities.

14. Explore the client's need for immediate and long-term financial or medical assistance.

15. Ascertain, through physical inspection of the client's premises, whether the

client's housing, financial, and emotional resources are adequate.

16. Refer the family members to appropriate social services to assist them in coping with financial hardships.

17. Follow up to determine the client's and family members' evaluation of the referral for social services.

18. Facilitate and monitor the client's and family members' follow-through on acquiring appropriate counseling and services.

19. Schedule regular contact with the family members to review the client's progress toward employment stability.

20. Reevaluate the client's goals, solutions, and strategies. Repeat steps where necessary.

—. _____
     _____

—. _____
     _____

—. _____
     _____

DIAGNOSTIC SUGGESTIONS

Axis I:	309.0	Adjustment Disorder With Depressed Mood
	309.24	Adjustment Disorder With Anxiety
	309.28	Adjustment Disorder With Mixed Anxiety and Depressed Mood

	296.xx	Major Depressive Disorder
	300.00	Anxiety Disorder NOS
	V62.2	Occupational Problem
	295.30	Schizophrenia, Paranoid Type
	295.10	Schizophrenia, Disorganized Type
	295.90	Schizophrenia, Undifferentiated Type
	298.9	Psychotic Disorder NOS
	296.xx	Bipolar I Disorder
	296.80	Bipolar Disorder NOS
	_____	_____
	_____	_____
Axis II:	301.0	Paranoid Personality Disorder
	301.20	Schizoid Personality Disorder
	301.22	Schizotypal Personality Disorder
	V71.09	No Diagnosis on Axis II
	799.9	Diagnosis Deferred on Axis II
	_____	_____
	_____	_____

FAMILY CONFLICT

BEHAVIORAL DEFINITIONS

1. Lack of conflict-resolution skills leads to frequent disparaging, arguing, and detachment.
2. Family members shun each other as a way of showing their anger.
3. Family members display a lack of cohesion and unity, with each member going in his/her own direction.
4. Serious disputes between members of the family remain unresolved.
5. Family members do not cooperate with one another.
6. Family conflict erupts into periodic physical confrontations.

—. _____

_____

—. _____

_____

—. _____

_____

LONG-TERM GOALS

1. Family members learn to resolve conflicts and accept individual differences.
2. Family members decrease the intensity and frequency of arguments among themselves.
3. Family members increase positive interactions among themselves.
4. Family members increase their cooperation and sense of unity.
5. Family members resolve serious disputes among themselves.

—. _____

     _____

—. _____

     _____

—. _____

     _____

SHORT-TERM OBJECTIVES

1. Describe the details regarding the nature, extent, and frequency of family conflicts. (1, 2)

2. Each family member rests assured of his/her safety. (1, 2, 3)

3. Identify the external stressors that contribute to tension within the family. (4)

4. Identify the interpersonal conflicts within the family that fracture the family unity. (5, 6)

5. Accept and follow through on referrals for services to reduce the level of stress within the family. (7)

6. Identify family strengths. (8)

7. Obtain instruction on the development of stress-reduction skills. (9)

8. Accept referrals for family therapy. (10, 11, 12, 13)

9. Identify recent conflict and steps that were taken to address and resolve it. (14)

THERAPEUTIC INTERVENTIONS

1. Provide an opportunity for each family member to express his/her view of family conflicts.

2. Assess for family violence.

3. Provide safe shelter options and referrals if family violence is determined.

4. Explore for external family stressors (e.g., financial stressors, lack of medical insurance, or lack of child care).

5. Probe the family members for interpersonal conflicts and grudges.

6. Ask each family member to list the most hurtful experience he/she has had within the family; assess as to whether pain and anger continue.

7. Provide referrals for services to reduce sources of external stress on the family (e.g., budget counseling, Medicaid, or child care programs).

8. Assist members in identifying family strengths that can be built on.

10. Cooperate in pursuing new conflict-resolution skills training. (13, 15)

11. Each family member describes the last enjoyable time spent in an activity together. (16)

12. Increase the frequency of enjoyable family experiences. (17, 18, 19)

13. Report a decrease in family conflict. (20)

__. _____
   _____

__. _____
   _____

__. _____
   _____

9. Provide referral for stress management classes to assist family members in increasing coping skills.

10. Educate family members regarding family therapy professionals in the community.

11. Assist the client in selecting a family therapist.

12. Obtain a written signed release of information to provide the family therapist with additional information at referral.

13. Provide referral and linkage to the family therapist.

14. Ask the family members to describe a recent conflict and explain how resolution was attempted; assess the effectiveness of the family's conflict-resolution skills.

15. Provide a referral for conflict-resolution skills training through specialized classes or focused family therapy.

16. Ask each family member to list the last positive experience that he/she has had within the family unit; assess for strengths and unity potential.

17. Assist each family member in identifying family activities he/she could participate in that would be pleasant and enjoyable.

18. Teach the principle of sacrificing personal pleasure at some times for the good of others within the family, ex-

pecting that at another time other family members will engage in an activity enjoyable to you.

19. Provide additional information on community resources available to the family members for recreation or pleasure.

20. Follow up with the family members to assess the nature, extent, and frequency of family conflicts and assess family's progress.

___. _____
    _____

___. _____
    _____

___. _____
    _____

DIAGNOSTIC SUGGESTIONS

Axis I:	300.4	Dysthymic Disorder
	311	Depressive Disorder NOS
	296.89	Bipolar II Disorder
	300.00	Anxiety Disorder NOS
	309.0	Adjustment Disorder With Depressed Mood
	309.24	Adjustment Disorder With Anxiety
	309.28	Adjustment Disorder With Mixed Anxiety and Depressed Mood
	_____	_____
	_____	_____
Axis II:	301.7	Antisocial Personality Disorder
	301.83	Borderline Personality Disorder
	301.9	Personality Disorder NOS
	V71.09	No Diagnosis on Axis II
	799.9	Diagnosis Deferred on Axis II
	_____	_____
	_____	_____

FOSTER CARE MALADJUSTMENT (CHILD)

BEHAVIORAL DEFINITIONS

1. Refuses to follow adult directives.
2. Exhibits frequent temper tantrums.
3. Uses obscenities to express anger or disdain.
4. Withdraws from social contact with peers and family members.
5. Cries frequently when frustrated, fearful, or hurt.
6. Eats too little or overeats.
7. Has difficulty sleeping.
8. Experiences frequent nightmares.
9. Has difficulty separating from caretakers.
10. Exhibits fear of new situations or any risk-taking activity.

—. _____
   _____
   _____
—. _____
   _____
   _____
—. _____
   _____

LONG-TERM GOALS

1. Follow adult directives.
2. Express anger in a controlled, respectful manner.
3. Interact socially with peers and family members.
4. Demonstrate appropriate eating habits.
5. Exhibit appropriate sleeping habits.
6. Exhibit appropriate independence for developmental level.
7. Express feelings openly but in a controlled, respectful manner.
8. Attend school on a consistent basis.

9. Return to the custody of biological parents when appropriate.
10. Accept the need for permanent placement away from the custody of biological parent.

—. _____

_____

—. _____

_____

—. _____

_____

SHORT-TERM OBJECTIVES

1. Child describes the perpetrator as well as the details of the nature, extent, and frequency of abuse or neglect. (1, 2)

2. Child attends supervised visitation with family if the court orders him/her to do so. (3, 4)

3. Foster parents attend parenting classes. (5, 6)

4. Foster parents verbalize an understanding of the consequences of abuse and neglect of children. (6)

5. Foster parents regularly attend counseling sessions to improve their stress-management skills. (7)

6. Foster parents utilize the services of respite care to obtain relief from child care responsibilities. (8)

7. Child attends group and/or individual counseling. (9, 10)

THERAPEUTIC INTERVENTIONS

1. Build rapport with the client through consistent eye contact, unconditional positive regard, warm acceptance, soft voice, conversation about nonthreatening topics, and expressions of reassurance regarding the child's safety.

2. Explore with the child and document abuse or neglect by all offenders.

3. Arrange for and supervise family visits with the child.

4. Write reports that elaborate on observation of the supervised family visits.

5. Refer foster parents to classes that teach effective parenting techniques.

6. Provide information to the parents regarding the short- and long-term effects of abuse and neglect on children.

7. Refer the foster parents to a support group and/or indi-

8. Child demonstrates expression of anger in a controlled manner. (9, 10, 11)

9. Child interacts socially with peers and family members. (9, 10, 12)

10. Child cooperates with an evaluation by a pediatrician. (13)

11. Child attends school consistently and demonstrates attentive, productive behavior in that setting. (14, 15)

—. _____
   _____

—. _____
   _____

—. _____
   _____

vidual counseling to learn to manage child care and other stress more effectively.

8. Link the foster parents with respite care programs in their area.

9. Refer the child to individual counseling.

10. Refer the child to group therapy with other foster children.

11. Monitor and reinforce the child's appropriate, controlled expression of anger.

12. Encourage and reinforce the child's social involvement with peers and foster family members.

13. Refer the child to a pediatrician to evaluate his/her physical health.

14. Obtain academic and behavioral reports from school regarding the child's performance.

15. Develop a plan conjointly with teacher, school counselor, individual counselor, and foster parents to address the child's behavioral, emotional, and academic needs.

—. _____
   _____

—. _____
   _____

—. _____
   _____

DIAGNOSTIC SUGGESTIONS

Axis I: 309.0   Adjustment Disorder With Depressed Mood
                309.24   Adjustment Disorder With Anxiety
                309.28   Adjustment Disorder With Mixed Anxiety and
                           Depressed Mood
                309.3   Adjustment Disorder With Disturbance of
                           Conduct
                309.4   Adjustment Disorder With Mixed Disturbance
                           of Emotions and Conduct
                309.9   Adjustment Disorder Unspecified
                309.21   Separation Anxiety Disorder
                312.81   Oppositional Defiant Disorder

                _____   _____

                _____   _____

Axis II: V71.09   No Diagnosis on Axis II
                799.9   Diagnosis Deferred on Axis II

                _____   _____

                _____   _____

HOMELESSNESS

BEHAVIORAL DEFINITIONS

1. Lack of shelter, regular meals, or clean clothing by an isolated person.
2. Lack of shelter, access to food, or clean clothing by several family members.
3. Lack of a place to sleep, find security, and escape from the elements other than a car, truck, or van.
4. Lack of access to adequate and nutritional meals.
5. Poverty resulting from unemployment.
6. Feelings of fear, shame, and depression.
7. Feelings of helplessness and hopelessness.
8. Pattern of chronic chemical dependence.
9. Intellectual capacity at the borderline level or lower.
10. Severe and persistent mental illness symptoms (e.g., hallucinations, delusions, mania, or major depression).

—. _____
   _____

—. _____
   _____

—. _____
   _____

LONG-TERM GOALS

1. Gain access to emergency shelter and nutritional food.
2. Move from living on the street through a continuum of supported residential opportunities to a more stable independent residence.
3. Decrease dependence on transitional living programs or shelters for the homeless.
4. Attain decreased behavioral concerns via stable medication use, supported by an increased level of motivation to stay healthy.
5. Acknowledge self as chemically dependent and begin to actively participate in a recovery program.
6. Access community-based social service programs that provide financial support and foster independence.

__. _____
   _____
__. _____
   _____
__. _____
   _____

SHORT-TERM OBJECTIVES

1. Stabilize current homelessness crisis. (1, 2, 3)
2. Describe history of homelessness. (4, 5)
3. Express emotions related to homelessness. (6, 7)
4. Identify barriers to maintaining long-term housing. (4, 5, 8)
5. Complete an application for appropriate subsidized housing. (9, 10)
6. Stabilize psychotic and other severe mental illness symptoms that interfere with maintaining a per-

THERAPEUTIC INTERVENTIONS

1. Refer the client to a local shelter for the homeless.
2. Coordinate funds for a crisis residential placement for the client (i.e., motel voucher or transitional program placement).
3. Facilitate placement of the client at the home of a family member, friend, or peer.
4. Request that the client describe his/her history of successful and problematic residential situations.
5. Direct the client to prepare a timeline of residences, pe-

sonal residence through the consistent use of psychotropic medication. (11, 12, 13)

7. Establish a mode of access to necessary medications despite the lack of a permanent residence or storage capacity. (11, 13, 14, 15, 16)

8. Report to an appropriate professional the side effects and effectiveness of prescribed medications. (12, 13, 17)

9. Verbalize desires and expectations regarding long-term plans for residence. (18, 19)

10. Cooperate with behavioral, cognitive, and medical evaluations to assess readiness for independent living. (20, 21, 22)

11. Obtain funding for residence. (23, 24, 25)

12. Implement a budget and banking routine to facilitate regular payment of rent or mortgage. (26, 27, 28)

13. Move from a more restrictive to less restrictive housing setting. (18, 29, 30, 31)

14. Describe the amount, frequency, and history of substance abuse. (32, 33)

15. Terminate substance abuse that interferes with the ability to maintain housing. (33, 34, 35)

16. Verbalize an understanding of legal rights related to housing for the mentally disabled. (36, 37)

riods of homelessness, and use of transitional housing. Process factors contributing to the client's lifestyle.

6. Explore the client's feelings associated with being homeless.

7. Provide the client with support and understanding regarding emotional concerns, acknowledging the natural emotions of frustration, discouragement, and embarrassment.

8. Ask the client to describe specific barriers he/she has experienced and/or expects in maintaining housing.

9. Assess the client's eligibility for government-subsidized housing programs (e.g., rent subsidies or reduced mortgage rates).

10. Assist the client in negotiating the application process for desired housing programs.

11. Arrange for a psychiatric evaluation and for a prescription for psychotropic medication, if necessary.

12. Educate the client about the use, possible side effects, and expected benefits of medication.

13. Monitor the client's medication compliance.

14. Store medications for the client in a safe, easily accessible facility.

15. Provide the homeless client with a smaller immediate supply of medication.

—. _____
   _____
—. _____
   _____
—. _____
   _____

16. Rent a secure storage space (e.g., locker or mailbox) in which the client may store necessary medications.

17. Monitor side effects of medication with the client and inform the medical staff.

18. Educate the client about the available options regarding the continuum of supports and services that are available for long-term housing.

19. Guide the client in developing a list of pros and cons for each of the housing options; provide the client with structure for making his/her own decision regarding housing.

20. Assess the client for danger to self and to others.

21. Assess the client's intellectual abilities as related to basic skills to maintain a home or refer the client for an assessment.

22. Coordinate a full medical evaluation to determine the client's physical care needs.

23. Assist the client in obtaining entitlements or other funding for general use.

24. Obtain specific subsidies that are available for assisting mentally ill or developmentally disabled individuals with housing.

25. Encourage and assist the client in obtaining regular employment to increase income that will defray housing costs (see Poverty in this Planner).

26. Assist the client in developing a budget for the payment of rent or mortgage.

27. Assist the client in obtaining a low-interest, no-fee bank account with a participating bank.

28. Obtain emergency funds for payment of the client's rent, mortgage, or utilities to prevent eviction.

29. Contact the discharge planning coordinator of the state inpatient or community psychiatric setting as early as possible in the client's treatment to coordinate discharge planning regarding housing.

30. Meet regularly with the incarcerated client to develop postrelease housing plans.

31. Coordinate ample visitation to a new, less restrictive setting in order for the client to become acquainted with the setting; be readily available to the client for questions and reassurance.

32. Gather a complete drug and alcohol history including amount and pattern of the client's use, signs and symptoms of use, and negative life consequences (social, legal, familial, and vocational).

33. Assist the client in identifying the impact of chemical dependence on his/her homelessness.

34. Refer the client to a chemi-

cal dependence detoxification treatment program.

35. Refer the client to Alcoholics Anonymous (AA), Narcotics Anonymous (NA), or other group-based abstinence programs.

36. Educate the client about tenant's rights (e.g., see *Renter's Rights* [Portman and Stewart]).

37. Coordinate contact with legal assistance programs if the client's rights continue to be violated.

—. _____
_____

—. _____
_____

—. _____
_____

DIAGNOSTIC SUGGESTIONS

Axis I:	297.1	Delusional Disorder
	295.xx	Schizophrenia
	295.10	Schizophrenia, Disorganized Type
	295.30	Schizophrenia, Paranoid Type
	295.90	Schizophrenia, Undifferentiated Type
	295.60	Schizophrenia, Residual Type
	295.70	Schizoaffective Disorder
	296.xx	Bipolar I Disorder
	296.89	Bipolar II Disorder
	V62.89	Phase of Life Problem
	_____	_____
	_____	_____
Axis II:	V71.09	No Diagnosis on Axis II
	799.9	Diagnosis Deferred on Axis II
	_____	_____
	_____	_____

HOUSING INADEQUACIES

BEHAVIORAL DEFINITIONS

1. The home has too many people crowded into a small living space.
2. The home lacks adequate privacy.
3. The home is inadequately furnished.
4. The home has inadequate heating and/or cooling.
5. The home is not clean or tidy.
6. Home repairs are not carried out promptly.
7. The home's sanitation is inadequate.
8. The home's living conditions are unsafe.
9. The family has moved several times within the past 5 years.

__. _____
   _____
__. _____
   _____
__. _____
   _____

LONG-TERM GOALS

1. Obtain housing that provides space for family members' functional living.
2. Obtain housing that provides adequate privacy.
3. Obtain furniture that is functional and adequate in terms of comfort, utility, and cleanliness.
4. Maintain permanent (over 5 years) residency.
5. Attain heating and cooling in the home that is adequate for reasonable comfort and safety.

6. Maintain the home with adequate standards of sanitation and safety.
7. Make home repairs within a reasonable time frame.

__. _____

_____

__. _____

_____

__. _____

_____

SHORT-TERM OBJECTIVES

1. Describe thoughts and feelings regarding current living arrangements. (1, 2)

2. Identify options for improving the family's housing situation. (3)

3. Develop and commit to a plan of increasing financial resources for housing improvement. (4)

4. Alter living arrangements to increase privacy for preadolescent and older family members. (2, 5)

5. Verbalize an understanding and implementation of safe and sanitary living arrangements. (2, 6, 7)

6. Obtain necessary home furnishings that provide for eating, sleeping, and other necessities of daily living. (2, 8, 9)

7. Identify feelings about and alternatives to living in the current neighborhood. (10, 11, 12)

THERAPEUTIC INTERVENTIONS

1. Assess the family members' perception of their current living arrangements/ conditions.

2. Observe the family in the home to determine the adequacy of the following: space and privacy for activities of daily living (ADL), comfort, safety, sanitation, and furnishings.

3. Discuss the need for and available options for housing improvements with the family members (e.g., moving to another location, appropriate social services, and self-help tools and ideas).

4. Explore with the family members the possibility of increasing financial resources through additional employment, social service assistance, educational training, and so on. Assist the family in setting goals for improvements.

8. Move to a more desirable neighborhood and into affordable housing that is more comfortable. (13, 14, 15)

9. Identify the repairs and maintenance needed for the home. (16)

10. Contact the landlord for necessary repairs and maintenance. (17, 18)

11. Make repairs and improvements to the home utilizing own initiative, skills, and resources. (19, 20)

12. Cooperate with periodic visits by caseworker to evaluate housing adequacy. (21)

__. _____
   _____

__. _____
   _____

__. _____
   _____

5. Assist the family members in making changes to the existing living arrangements to ensure reasonable privacy (e.g., room partitions, rearrangement of furniture, or new bedroom assignments).

6. Assess the family members' knowledge and practice of home safety and sanitation.

7. Teach the family members basic principles and practices of home sanitation and safety; assist the family in setting goals and making plans to correct deficits.

8. Discuss options for improving and/or acquiring necessary home furnishings. Assist the family members in identifying resources for free or very reasonably priced new or used furnishings.

9. Facilitate the family's obtaining furnishings and moving them into the home.

10. Discuss with the family members their assessment of their neighborhood, including a discussion of safety and the proximity to employment, medical services, school, and the social support network.

11. Explore with the family members their feelings about moving to a more satisfactory neighborhood.

12. Assist the family members in identifying subsidized

housing alternatives that they may find more safe and satisfying than their current living situation.

13. Facilitate the family members' applying for funds and/or housing for which they qualify.

14. Facilitate and monitor the family's moving to a more convenient, safe, satisfactory neighborhood.

15. Support the family members' desires and efforts to improve the current condition of their housing.

16. Assist the family members in listing the repairs or improvements that could and should be made to current housing.

17. Encourage and reinforce the parents in asserting themselves to the landlord in requesting the needed repairs or improvements to the property.

18. Teach the parents about their rights as renters to obtain safe and sanitary conditions from the landlord; facilitate their contact with community agencies that will advocate for tenants.

19. Encourage and reinforce family members in using their own skills to repair and improve their housing.

20. Facilitate the parents' obtaining finances and subsidized building materials for the necessary repairs.

21. Monitor the safety, cleanliness, and adequacy of the housing for the family through periodic follow-up visits.

—. _____

_____

—. _____

_____

—. _____

_____

DIAGNOSTIC SUGGESTIONS

Axis I:	309.0	Adjustment Disorder With Depressed Mood
	309.24	Adjustment Disorder With Anxiety
	309.28	Adjustment Disorder With Mixed Anxiety and Depressed Mood
	296.xx	Major Depressive Disorder
	300.00	Anxiety Disorder NOS
	V62.2	Occupational Problem
	295.30	Schizophrenia, Paranoid Type
	295.10	Schizophrenia, Disorganized Type
	295.90	Schizophrenia, Undifferentiated Type
	298.9	Psychotic Disorder NOS
	296.xx	Bipolar I Disorder
	296.80	Bipolar Disorder NOS
	_____	_____
	_____	_____
Axis II:	301.0	Paranoid Personality Disorder
	301.20	Schizoid Personality Disorder
	301.22	Schizotypal Personality Disorder
	V71.09	No Diagnosis on Axis II
	799.9	Diagnosis Deferred on Axis II
	_____	_____
	_____	_____

JUVENILE DELINQUENCY

BEHAVIORAL DEFINITIONS

1. Refuses to follow adult directives and is disrespectful to authority figures.
2. Steals and engages in other unlawful behavior that has led to arrests.
3. Threatens others or has engaged in assaultive behavior.
4. Does not respect the rights, feelings, or needs of others.
5. Belongs to a gang that protects turf and encourages violence.
6. Lies and projects blame for his/her misbehavior onto others.
7. Has a history of setting fires or damaging property in other acts of anger or revenge.
8. Is often truant from school and lacks motivation to succeed academically.
9. Has a learning disability.
10. Abuses drugs and/or alcohol.
11. Has been cruel to people and/or animals.
12. Has used a weapon to confront others.
13. Has run away from home overnight at least twice.
14. Has been arrested or adjudicated as being in need of supervision.
15. Has parents who enforce household rules inconsistently.
16. Has parents whose enforcement of household rules is too strict or too lax, fluctuating between abuse and neglect.
17. Has parents or caregivers who use corporal punishment regularly.

—. _____
   _____

—. _____
   _____

—. _____
   _____

LONG-TERM GOALS

1. Terminate all illegal and antisocial behaviors.
2. Demonstrate increased honesty, compliance with rules, sensitivity to the feelings and rights of others, control over impulses, and acceptance of responsibility for behavior.
3. Demonstrate empathy, concern, and sensitivity for the thoughts, feelings, and needs of others.
4. Learn anger-management skills and terminate assaultive behavior.
5. Attend school and show respect for the rules and authority figures.
6. Accept responsibility for own actions, including apologizing for hurts and not blaming others.
7. Come to an understanding and acceptance of the need for limits and boundaries on behavior.
8. Parents develop appropriate expectations about adolescent behavior.
9. Parents learn appropriate methods to nurture, guide, and discipline children.

—. _____

_____

—. _____

_____

—. _____

_____

SHORT-TERM OBJECTIVES	THERAPEUTIC INTERVENTIONS
1. Admit to illegal or maladaptive behavior that has violated the law and/or the rights and feelings of others. (1, 2, 3)	1. Gather a history of the client's delinquent behavior.
	2. Emphasize the reality of increasingly negative consequences if the client's continued delinquency occurs.
2. Identify relationships that have been damaged because of disrespect, disloyalty, aggression, or dishonesty. (4, 5)	3. Confront the client's lack of taking responsibility for his/her behavior.
3. Agree to make restitution to those who have been harmed by own actions. (5, 6)	4. Ask the client to list those people he/she has hurt emotionally and/or physically.

4. Verbalize an understanding of the legal consequences of own antisocial behavior. (2, 7)

5. List the negative consequences that have resulted from poor anger management. (8)

6. Describe alternative, constructive ways to manage anger. (9, 10)

7. Provide restitution to those who have been victims of own antisocial behavior. (11, 12)

8. Attend school on a consistent basis. (13, 14)

9. Parents verbalize an understanding of typical adolescent behavior. (15)

10. Parents define reasonable rules that will be consistently enforced. (16, 17, 19)

11. Parents implement positive and negative reinforcement, punishment, shaping, time-out, and stimulus control to influence the client's behavior. (18, 19)

12. Family members attend counseling to learn conflict-resolution, communication, and boundary establishment techniques. (20, 21)

—. _____
    _____

—. _____
    _____

—. _____
    _____

5. Confront lack of sensitivity to the needs and feelings of others.

6. Develop a plan with the client whereby he/she provides restitution to those who have suffered from his/her behaviors.

7. Explain to the client the legal consequences of his/her antisocial behavior and describe the process and people involved in the court proceedings.

8. Point out instances of the client's uncontrolled, aggressive, impulsive, disrespectful expressions of anger and assist him/her in listing the negative consequences of this behavior for himself/herself and others.

9. Role-play situations that have prompted uncontrolled anger expression by the client and substitute anger-management techniques (e.g., deep breathing, time out, relaxation, and positive self-talk) at critical times in the interaction.

10. Refer the client to individual or group counseling to learn anger-management techniques.

11. Arrange for the client to engage in community service or other employment to earn money for restitution to his/her victims.

12. Monitor client's follow-through on making restitution to his/her victims.

13. Establish procedures whereby school will track client's attendance daily and notify caseworker and parents if truancy occurs.

14. Contract with the client that he/she will attend school consistently.

15. Provide information to the parents regarding typical adolescent behaviors.

16. Help the parents define and clarify household rules.

17. Provide information to the parents regarding the use of consequences and rewards to manage the client's behavior.

18. Teach parents the principles of behavior modification as used in such techniques as shaping behavior, time-out, positive reinforcement, negative reinforcement, and punishment.

19. Refer parents to classes teaching effective parenting methods.

20. Teach the family what to expect from family counseling to reduce anxiety and resistance.

21. Refer the family for counseling to a community or private agency; monitor follow-through.

—. _____
_____
_____

—. _____
_____
_____

—. _____
_____

DIAGNOSTIC SUGGESTIONS

Axis I: 312.8   Conduct Disorder
313.81   Oppositional Defiant Disorder
312.9   Disruptive Behavior Disorder NOS
314.01   Attention Deficit/Hyperactivity Disorder,
Predominantly Hyperactive-Impulsive Type
315.9   Learning Disorder NOS
303.90   Alcohol Dependence
305.00   Alcohol Abuse
304.30   Cannabis Dependence
305.20   Cannabis Abuse
304.80   Polysubstance Dependence
_____   _____
_____   _____

Axis II: V71.09   No Diagnosis on Axis II
_____   _____
_____   _____

JUVENILE RUNAWAY

BEHAVIORAL DEFINITIONS

1. Leaves home overnight or longer without permission.
2. Is homeless as a result of runaway behavior.
3. Resides in inadequate and/or dangerous living space.
4. Lacks adequate economic support.
5. Lacks an adequate food supply.
6. Engages in theft or other dangerous activities to support self.
7. Abuses alcohol and/or drugs.
8. Engages in prostitution to support self.
9. Is lonely, depressed, and afraid.
10. Has history of severe family conflict based in abuse and/or neglect.
11. Allows self to be used sexually in exchange for food, shelter, and/or drugs.

__. _____
_____

__. _____
_____

__. _____
_____

LONG-TERM GOALS

1. Obtain adequate, safe housing, health care, and food access.
2. Terminate illegal and/or dangerous activities.
3. Terminate use of alcohol and/or drugs.
4. Parents stop physical, sexual, emotional, and verbal abuse and/or neglect of the client.

5. Return home with supportive counseling focused on family problems.
6. Follow household rules, showing respect for authority and bonding with the family.
7. Parents develop appropriate parenting skills and treat the client with respect and kindness.

—. _____
   _____

—. _____
   _____

—. _____
   _____

SHORT-TERM OBJECTIVES

1. Cooperate with a referral to a physician for a health assessment. (1)

2. Accept referral for drug and alcohol evaluation and treatment. (2)

3. Agree to placement in community-supported safe housing or shelter. (3)

4. Describe the nature, extent, frequency, and perpetrators of abuse or neglect. (4, 5, 6)

5. Express feelings of pain and anger resulting from the abuse or neglect. (4, 5, 7)

6. Express feelings about the perpetrator, placing clear responsibility on him/her for the abuse. (7, 8)

7. Admit to illegal or antisocial behavior. (9, 10, 11)

8. Parents verbalize expectations for age-appropriate

THERAPEUTIC INTERVENTIONS

1. Refer the client to a physician to rule out any medical conditions that are in need of immediate treatment.

2. Refer the client to a drug and alcohol counselor for an evaluation for chemical dependence.

3. Locate adequate housing or shelter for the client and facilitate immediate placement.

4. Built rapport with the client through consistent eye contact, unconditional positive regard, warm acceptance, soft voice, conversation about nonthreatening topics, and expressions of reassurance regarding his/her safety.

5. Slowly explore the factual details of any abuse experiences without pressing the

behavior for the client. (12, 13)

9. Parents indicate a need and desire to learn skills to manage children's behavior. (14, 15, 16, 17)

10. Parents attend classes to learn parenting skills. (17)

11. Parents implement social and recreational activities, cognitive restructuring, and deep muscle relaxation techniques to reduce tension. (18, 19)

12. Implement social, recreational, and therapeutic activities to reduce stress in a prosocial manner. (20)

13. Identify problems, generate solutions, and choose the best solution. (21, 22, 23)

14. Parents and client demonstrate understanding of effective communication skills. (23, 24, 25)

15. Parents and client identify and express their feelings appropriately. (26, 27)

—. _____

 _____

—. _____

 _____

—. _____

 _____

client beyond his/her level of trust.

6. Report child abuse to proper authorities in conjunction with legal mandate.

7. Facilitate the client's expression of feelings of pain, shame, rage, and fear associated with his/her abuse experiences.

8. Confront the client for excusing the perpetrator and reinforce all statements that place clear responsibility on the perpetrator for the abuse or neglect.

9. Explore the client's history of antisocial behavior, noting whether illegal activity began before running away or was triggered by desperate conditions.

10. Emphasize the negative consequences and danger to the client of continuing delinquency.

11. Assess the client's attitude regarding illegal and antisocial activity (e.g., remorse, callousness, bravado, or rebellion).

12. Provide information about typical adolescent behaviors and correct parents' unreasonable expectations for their child.

13. Assess the parents' childhood as to whether they were subjected to abuse, neglect, or unreasonable expectations; point out the

need to not repeat the cycle with their children.

14. Provide the parents with information about the benefits of enforcing rules consistently.

15. Urge the parents to read books on effective parenting techniques.

16. Provide information to the parents regarding the effective use of consequences and rewards to manage children's behavior.

17. Refer the parents to community-based parenting classes to increase their skills and understanding in dealing with their children.

18. Help the parents develop a behavioral coping plan for their personal relaxation (e.g., enjoyable discussions, physical exercise, social engagements, and recreational activities).

19. Teach the parents relaxation techniques (e.g., deep breathing, and muscle relaxation) as a means of reducing stress and irritability.

20. Teach the client behavioral techniques to manage stress (e.g., keeping a journal, listening to or playing music, engaging in exercise, deep muscle relaxation, calling a friend, or talking to a counselor).

21. Assist the client in identifying current problems that

generate tension and con-
flict.

22. Provide the client with information on steps of effective problem solving (e.g.,
identify problem, brain-
storm possible solutions,
evaluate the pros and cons
of each solution, and select
best solution).

23. Use role-playing, modeling,
and behavioral rehearsal to
allow the client to practice
problem-solving and/or communication skills; give feedback, redirection, and
reinforcement as indicated.

24. Teach the parents and the
client effective, respectful
communication that uses "I"
messages.

25. Assist the client and the
parents in learning social
skills (e.g., eye contact, appropriate greetings, pleasant and respectful
conversation, and showing
interest in others).

26. Teach the family members
to identify feelings and
allow each person to freely
express those feelings
within the boundaries of
mutual respect.

27. Assign the family members
to keep individual journals
of events and feelings with
the understanding that the
written material will be
shared in future sessions;
process the material care-
fully to promote under-

standing between family members.

—. _____

_____

—. _____

_____

—. _____

_____

DIAGNOSTIC SUGGESTIONS

Axis I:

309.0	Adjustment Disorder With Depressed Mood
309.3	Adjustment Disorder With Disturbance of Conduct
309.4	Adjustment Disorder With Mixed Disturbance of Emotions and Conduct
313.81	Oppositional Defiant Disorder
V61.21	Sexual Abuse of Child
995.53	Sexual Abuse of Child (Victim)
V61.20	Parent–Child Relational Problem
_____	_____
_____	_____

Axis II:

V71.09	No Diagnosis on Axis II
_____	_____
_____	_____

LEGAL INVOLVEMENT

BEHAVIORAL DEFINITIONS

1. Appealing a court decision.
2. Being sued.
3. Suing someone else.
4. Being involved in a criminal proceeding.
5. Being in jail or in prison.
6. Being on probation.
7. Being on parole.
8. Being involved in a child custody dispute.
9. Being involved in a legal separation or divorce proceedings.

___. _____

_____

___. _____

_____

___. _____

_____

LONG-TERM GOALS

1. The appeal of a court decision is initiated and resolved.
2. A suit against the client is resolved.
3. The suit against another party is resolved.
4. A criminal proceeding is resolved.
5. Client is released from jail.
6. Client is released from probation.
7. Client is released from parole.
8. Child custody dispute is resolved in the best interest of the child.

9. Legal separation or divorce proceeding is resolved in the best interest of both parties.
10. Family is functional during period of probation, parole, or incarceration.
11. Family is reunited following client's release from probation, parole, or incarceration.
12. Family is functional following client's release from probation, parole, or incarceration.

—. _____

_____

—. _____

_____

—. _____

_____

SHORT-TERM OBJECTIVES

1. The client verbalizes an understanding of the nature of the issues surrounding the lawsuit or criminal proceeding against him/her. (1)
2. The client and family members report that their social, emotional, and financial needs are met during the course of the lawsuit or criminal proceeding against the client. (2, 3, 4)
3. The client and family members verbalize an understanding of the nature and details of the jail sentence. (5)
4. The client and family members report that their social, emotional, and financial needs are met during the client's or family member's

THERAPEUTIC INTERVENTIONS

1. Explain the nature of the lawsuit or criminal proceedings against the client and discuss the options for resolution with the client and family members.
2. Facilitate the client's securing appropriate legal services to initiate appropriate steps to resolve the lawsuit or criminal proceedings.
3. Assess the client's and family members' need for social, emotional, and financial support during the lawsuit or criminal proceedings against the client.
4. Explain, initiate, and/or facilitate options for social, emotional, or financial support during a lawsuit or criminal proceeding against the client.

period of probation, parole, or incarceration. (6)

5. The child is provided with necessary physical care and emotional nurturance during his/her caretaker's absence. (7, 8, 9)

6. The family members are reunited and mutually supportive following incarceration. (10, 11)

7. The client and family members verbalize an understanding of the process of removal from probation or parole. (12)

8. The client verbalizes an understanding of the appeals process and an awareness of the pros and cons of filing an appeal. (13)

9. The client and family members report that their social, emotional, and financial needs are met during the appeals process. (14, 15, 16)

10. The client verbalizes an understanding of the process and the pros and cons of initiating a lawsuit against another party. (17)

11. The client and family members report that their social, emotional, and financial needs are met during the course of the lawsuit against another party. (18, 19)

12. The client and family members agree to resolve the custody dispute in the best interest of the child. (20)

5. Explain to the client and family members the nature and details of the jail sentence.

6. Explain, initiate, and/or facilitate options for social, emotional, or financial support during the probation, parole, or jail sentence.

7. Facilitate arrangements for child care or custody during the client's or family member's period of probation, parole, or incarceration.

8. Explain to the child the reason and arrangements for his/her care during the caretaker's probation, parole, or incarceration.

9. Provide emotional support to the child and/or other family members during the period of probation, parole, or incarceration.

10. Facilitate reunion of family members and hold a family session to allow for expression of hopes, fears, and other feelings.

11. Monitor family functioning following incarceration. Observe for signs of physical and/or emotional abuse, adequacy of personal and financial resources, and so on (see Neglect of Child and Partner Abuse in this Planner).

12. Explain the process of the client's or family member's removal from probation or release from parole.

13. The child understands and accepts the terms of the custody arrangements. (21, 22)

14. The child reports no abuse or neglect during custody dispute between parents. (23)

15. The client and spouse agree to file for separation or divorce. (24, 25)

16. The client, spouse, and/or children verbalize an understanding of the process and implications of separation or divorce for each family member. (24, 26, 27)

17. The family members report that their social, emotional, and financial needs are met during and after the divorce proceedings. (27, 28, 29)

18. The children report being well cared for following the divorce proceedings. (30, 31, 32)

___. _____
    _____
___. _____
    _____
___. _____
    _____

13. Discuss with the client the stages of the appeals process. Explain the pros and cons of the appeals process.

14. Facilitate the client's securing appropriate legal services to initiate the appeals process.

15. Assess the client's need for social, emotional, and financial support during the appeals process.

16. Explain, initiate, and/or facilitate options for social, emotional, and financial support during the appeals process.

17. Discuss the nature of the client's lawsuit against another party and discuss options for resolution with the client and family members.

18. Assess the client's and family members' need for social, emotional, and financial support during the client's lawsuit against another party.

19. Explain, initiate, and/or facilitate options for social, emotional, or financial support during a lawsuit against another party.

20. Solicit agreement from both parents that they will work for a custody settlement that is in the best interest of the child and is not based in their marital conflicts or animosities.

21. Explain to the child the reasons and arrangements for

his/her care during the custody dispute.

22. Provide emotional support to the child and/or other family members during the period of the custody dispute.

23. Monitor the family members' functioning during and following the custody dispute. Observe for signs of physical and/or emotional abuse, adequacy of personal and financial resources, and so on (see Neglect of Child and Partner Abuse in this Planner).

24. Discuss with the client and his/her spouse the stages of the process of filing for legal separation or divorce. Explain the pros and cons of legal separation or divorce.

25. Facilitate the client's securing appropriate legal services to initiate the legal separation or divorce.

26. Meet with the children to explain the divorce proceedings and to allow a sharing of feelings.

27. Meet with the parents and children to allow the parents to explain divorce and reassure the children of their care.

28. Assess the need for social, emotional, or financial support for the couple and children during the legal separation or divorce process.

29. Explain, initiate, and/or facilitate options for social, emotional, and financial support during the legal separation or divorce process.

30. Observe the family members' functioning during and following the legal separation or divorce. Observe for signs of physical and/or emotional abuse, adequacy of personal and financial resources, and so on (see Neglect of Child and Partner Abuse in this Planner).

31. Explain to the child the reason and arrangements for his/her care following the legal separation or divorce process.

32. Provide emotional support to the child during and following the legal separation or divorce.

—. _____
   _____

—. _____
   _____

—. _____
   _____

DIAGNOSTIC SUGGESTIONS

Axis I:	309.0	Adjustment Disorder With Depressed Mood
	309.24	Adjustment Disorder With Anxiety
	V71.01	Adult Antisocial Behavior
	309.3	Adjustment Disorder With Disturbance of Conduct
	_____	_____
	_____	_____

Axis II: 301.7   Antisocial Personality Disorder
                301.0   Paranoid Personality Disorder

                _____   _____

                _____   _____

MURDER VICTIM'S FAMILY

BEHAVIORAL DEFINITIONS

1. Preoccupation with the family member's murder coupled with poor concentration, tearful spells, and confusion about the future.
2. A sense of rage and desire for revenge focused on the perpetrator of the murder.
3. Disturbing dreams or intrusive thoughts associated with the murder.
4. Feelings of guilt or an unreasonable belief of having contributed to the death of the significant other.
5. Lack of appetite, weight loss, and/or insomnia.
6. Excessive and persistent worry about several life circumstances that has no factual or logical basis.
7. Symptoms of hypervigilence such as feeling constantly on edge, concentration difficulties, trouble falling asleep, and general state of irritability.
8. A sense of detachment or isolation from others.
9. A pessimistic, fatalistic attitude regarding the future.
10. Alcohol and/or drug abuse.
11. Inability to maintain employment due to anger, depression, and/or anxiety symptoms.

___. _____
    _____
___. _____
    _____
___. _____
    _____

LONG-TERM GOALS

1. Accept the loss, resolve uncontrolled anger, and resume normal functioning while grieving.
2. Begin a healthy grieving process.
3. Reduce overall level, frequency, and intensity of anxiety and depression so that daily functioning is not impaired.
4. Develop and implement effective coping skills to carry out normal responsibilities and participate constructively in relationships.
5. Terminate the destructive behaviors and implement behaviors that promote healing, acceptance of the past events, and responsible living.

—. _____

_____

—. _____

_____

—. _____

_____

SHORT-TERM OBJECTIVES	THERAPEUTIC INTERVENTIONS
1. Tell as much of the story of the murder as can comfortably be shared. (1, 2)	1. Actively build trust with the family members through eye contact, active listening, unconditional positive regard, and expressions of reassurance regarding the client's safety.
2. Share feelings of shock, devastation, grief, and anger associated with the death of the loved one. (1, 3)	
3. Verbalize thoughts and feelings about the perpetrator of the murder. (1, 4)	2. Ask the family members to elaborate on the circumstances of the murder.
4. Acknowledge the need to control the desire for revenge. (4, 5)	3. Allow the family members to share their individual emotional reactions to the loss of the loved one.
5. Verbalize an understanding of the steps of the grieving process. (6)	4. Explore the family members' thoughts and feelings associated with the perpetrator.
6. Read books on the topic of grief to better understand	

the experience and increase a sense of hope. (7)

7. Accept referral to individual or family counseling. (8)

8. Accept referral to a grief or victim support group for families. (9)

9. Verbalize an understanding of the legal process of police investigation and court proceedings. (10, 11)

10. Cooperate with legal authorities under the guidance of an attorney. (12, 13)

11. Describe the amount, history, and frequency of substance abuse used to cope with the trauma. (14)

12. Identify the negative consequences of substance abuse. (15, 16)

13. Accept referral to alcohol and/or drug evaluation and treatment. (17)

14. Identify sources of support among extended family and friends. (8, 9, 17)

15. Report as to success at receiving emotional support from others. (18)

16. Utilize spiritual faith and spiritual leaders as sources of comfort and hope. (19, 20, 21)

___. _____
    _____

___. _____
    _____

___. _____
    _____

5. Assess for uncontrolled rage toward the perpetrator; attempt to diffuse the anger through active, compassionate listening while setting limits on reactivity.

6. Educate the family members on the stages of the grieving process.

7. Ask the family members to read books on grieving and loss (e.g., *Good Grief: A Constructive Approach to the Problem of Loss* [Westberg] and *The Grief Recovery Handbook: The Action Program for Moving Beyond Death, Divorce, and Other Losses* [James and Friedman]).

8. Refer the client and family members to individual or family counseling.

9. Refer the family members to a grief and loss or victim's support group.

10. Explain the legal process that will ensue due to the murder.

11. Refer the family members to a community-based victim's advocacy service.

12. Encourage cooperation with the police investigation of the murder but provide the family with referrals to legal representation.

13. Refer the family to a legal aid agency for counsel regarding the legal proceedings.

14. Gather data from the family members regarding the

amount, history, and frequency of their substance abuse as a means of coping with the feelings of grief and anger.

15. Teach the family members the negative consequences of abusing substances as a means of coping with grief, guilt, or anger (e.g., exacerbation of negative emotions; reduction of inhibition to irrational impulses; precipitation of legal, vocational, and relational problems; and precipitation of a pattern of chemical dependence).

16. Ask each adult and adolescent family member to commit to suffering through the grief with support but without substance abuse.

17. Ask each family member to specifically identify people that he/she can turn to for understanding and support; brainstorm with the family members regarding any additional supportive individuals they could rely on in this crisis.

18. Assist the family members in developing concrete plans for reaching out to seek support from understanding persons; monitor their follow-through with these plans in order to prevent their social withdrawal.

19. Explore the family members' spiritual beliefs and practices as potential sources of support.

20. Encourage the family members to rely upon their spiritual faith, promises, activities (e.g., prayer, meditation, worship, and music) and fellowship as sources of support.

21. Facilitate contact between the family members and their spiritual leaders or support persons.

__. _____

_____

__. _____

_____

__. _____

_____

DIAGNOSTIC SUGGESTIONS

Axis I:	V62.82	Bereavement
	309.0	Adjustment Disorder With Depressed Mood
	309.24	Adjustment Disorder With Anxiety
	309.3	Adjustment Disorder With Disturbance of Conduct
	_____	_____
	_____	_____
Axis II:	V71.09	No Diagnosis on Axis II
	799.9	Diagnosis Deferred on Axis II
	_____	_____
	_____	_____

NEGATIVE PEER GROUP (ADOLESCENT)

BEHAVIORAL DEFINITIONS

1. Interacts with negative, inappropriate peers.
2. Engages in illegal and/or antisocial behavior with peer group.
3. Defends turf and initiates altercations with peer group.
4. Refuses to follow adult directives and challenges all authority figures.
5. Comes from a household where rules are inconsistent, too lax, or too strict.
6. Does not attend school and/or leaves school during school hours without permission.
7. Abuses alcohol and/or drugs with peer group.
8. Leaves home overnight or longer without permission.

___. _____
_____
___. _____
_____
___. _____
_____

LONG-TERM GOALS

1. Interact with appropriate, positive peers.
2. Terminate illegal and/or dangerous activities.
3. Follow household rules, showing respect for authority and bonding with family.
4. Attend school regularly.
5. Terminate use of alcohol and/or drugs.

6. Parents develop appropriate parenting skills and treat the client with respect and kindness.

__. _____

_____

__. _____

_____

__. _____

_____

SHORT-TERM OBJECTIVES

1. Describe friends, their values, and types of activities engaged in together. (1, 2, 3, 4)
2. Admit to illegal or antisocial behavior that has violated the law and/or the rights and feelings of others. (5, 6, 7)
3. Follow household rules. (8, 9, 10)
4. Parents improve parenting skills. (11, 12, 13)
5. Describe the history and pattern of alcohol and drug use. (14)
6. Accept referral for drug and/or alcohol evaluation and treatment. (15)
7. Identify stress-related problems, generate solutions, and choose the best solution. (16, 17, 18)
8. Demonstrate improved social skills. (18, 19)
9. Parents and the client demonstrate an understanding of effective communication skills. (20, 21)

THERAPEUTIC INTERVENTIONS

1. Construct with the client a sociogram of his/her social network, identifying the degree of closeness of each friend and their interrelationship.
2. Explore with the client his/her values and priorities as well as those of his/her friends.
3. Assist the client in identifying why he/she has chosen specific peers to be his/her friend.
4. Explore the leisure activities enjoyed by the client's peer group; assess for constructivity and legality.
5. Emphasize the reality of negative consequences for the client if maladaptive behavior continues.
6. Confront the client's lack of sensitivity to the needs and feelings of others.
7. Help the client provide restitution to those who have suffered from his/her behaviors.

10. Learn how to manage anger. (22, 23)

11. Attend school classes consistently. (24, 25, 26)

12. Initiate contact with a positive peer for a constructive activity. (27, 28, 29)

13. Attend a community-based activity center for teens. (30, 31)

__. _____

_____

__. _____

_____

__. _____

_____

8. Provide the parents with information about the benefits of enforcing rules consistently.

9. Set firm limits on the client as to complying with household rules and societal laws; clearly identify the negative consequences of continuing to break rules and/or laws.

10. Reinforce the client's compliance with the rules and laws.

11. Urge the parents to read books on effective parenting techniques (e.g., *Toughlove* [Wachel, York, and York] or *Family Rules* [Kaye]).

12. Provide information to the parents regarding the effective use of consequences and rewards to manage children's behavior.

13. Refer the parents to community-based parenting classes to increase their skills and understanding in dealing with their children.

14. Gather a history of the client's drug and alcohol abuse.

15. Refer the client to a drug and alcohol counselor for an evaluation and treatment of chemical dependence.

16. Assist the client in identifying current problems that generate stress and conflict.

17. Assist the client with information on steps of effective problem solving (e.g., identify the problem, brainstorm possible solutions, evaluate

the pros and cons of each solution, and select the best solution).

18. Use role-playing, modeling, and behavioral rehearsal to allow the client to practice problem-solving and social skills; give feedback, redirection, and reinforcement as indicated.

19. Assist the client in learning social skills (e.g., eye contact, appropriate greetings, pleasant respectful conversation, and showing interest in others).

20. Teach the parents and the client effective, respectful communication that uses "I" messages.

21. Teach family members to identify feelings and allow each person to freely express those feelings within the boundaries of mutual respect.

22. Teach the client and parents behavioral techniques to manage anger and stress (e.g., keeping a journal, listening to or playing music, exercise, deep muscle relaxation, or talking to a counselor).

23. Explore the client's experiences and hurts that have led to anger; refer for counseling.

24. Develop a contract with the client to attend all school classes regularly.

25. Monitor and reinforce the client's school attendance.

26. Outline the negative consequences of continued school truancy.

27. Assist the client in identifying three positive peers who have good values and a responsible lifestyle.

28. Ask the client to list constructive social activities that could be enjoyed with positive peers.

29. Assign the client to initiate contact with a positive peer and plan a constructive activity together.

30. Refer the client to a community-based teen center for supervised, constructive activity.

31. Accompany and monitor the client's attendance at the teen center.

—. _____
   _____
   _____

—. _____
   _____

—. _____
   _____

DIAGNOSTIC SUGGESTIONS

Axis I:	313.81	Oppositional Defiant Disorder
	312.8	Conduct Disorder
	312.9	Disruptive Behavioral Disorder NOS
	V61.20	Parent–Child Relational Problem
	_____	_____
	_____	_____
Axis II:	V71.09	No Diagnosis on Axis II
	_____	_____
	_____	_____

NEGLECT OF CHILD

BEHAVIORAL DEFINITIONS

1. An adult member of the family fails to ensure that children are clean, well fed, adequately clothed, and supervised.
2. Children do not receive a balanced diet.
3. Children do not receive enough food.
4. Children are inappropriately dressed for the weather.
5. Children do not have an appropriate place to sleep.
6. Children do not receive regular immunizations.
7. Children do not receive immediate, appropriate medical care when they are seriously sick.
8. Children are inappropriately tired and sleepy and are poorly groomed.
9. Children are too frequently sick or injured.

__. _____

_____

__. _____

_____

__. _____

_____

LONG-TERM GOALS

1. Parents accept the responsibility to provide normal care and nurturance to their children.
2. Children receive adequate care and nurturance to support their physical, emotional, and social growth and development.
3. Children are clean, appropriately dressed, and well groomed.
4. Children are provided adequate food and balanced diets.

5. Children receive adequate sleep.
6. Children receive appropriate immunizations according to schedule.
7. Children receive appropriate routine medical care.
8. Children receive timely and appropriate medical care when sick or injured.

—. _____

   _____

—. _____

   _____

—. _____

   _____

SHORT-TERM OBJECTIVES

1. Parents verbalize and maintain standards for appropriate dress and cleanliness for their child. (1, 2, 3, 4)

2. Parents verbalize a knowledge of an adequate and age-appropriate diet for the child. (5, 6)

3. Parents provide their children with a balanced nutritional diet. (7, 8)

4. Parents demonstrate sufficient financial and food resources to ensure an adequate diet for their child. (9, 10)

5. Parents verbalize an understanding of appropriate sleep patterns for their child. (11, 12)

6. Parents provide a physical environment and appropriate behavioral management

THERAPEUTIC INTERVENTIONS

1. Ascertain the parents' level of knowledge regarding standards of dress and grooming for the child.

2. Observe the child in the home and other environments to determine the adequacy of the parents' application of reasonable standards of dress and grooming.

3. Discuss with the parents any deficits in their standards of dress and grooming for the child and assist in correcting them.

4. Facilitate parental follow-through on enacting reasonable standards of dress and grooming for the child; process any barriers to this enactment and provide resources for follow-through.

to ensure adequate sleep for their child. (13, 14)

7. Parents verbalize an understanding of the necessity for appropriate immunizations for their child and schedule immunizations accordingly. (15, 16)

8. Parents obtain immunizations for their child. (16, 17)

9. Parents have sufficient resources to ensure routine medical care for their child. (9, 18)

10. Parents schedule appropriate routine medical care for their child. (17, 18, 19)

11. Parents verbalize an understanding of the physical, emotional, and social needs of their child at each developmental stage. (20, 21, 22)

12. Parents provide a physical, emotional, and social environment for their child that supports adequate growth and development. (23, 24, 25)

13. Parents verbalize an understanding of the symptoms of an acute or chronic disease in their child. (26, 27)

14. Parents respond appropriately to symptoms of acute or chronic disease or injury in their child. (28, 29)

___. _____
   _____

___. _____
   _____

___. _____
   _____

5. Ascertain the parents' level of knowledge regarding a balanced and age-appropriate diet for the child.

6. Discuss with the parents any deficits in the child's diet and assist in making plans to correct them (e.g., make referrals to the county health department nutritionist, the Women, Infants, and Children [WIC] program, and the school lunch program).

7. Observe the child in the home and other environments to determine the adequacy of his/her diet.

8. Monitor and encourage the parents' implementation of a balanced nutritional diet for the child; redirect when necessary.

9. Review the parents' economic resources to ensure that they are adequate to provide for the basic needs of the family (e.g., food, medical care, clothing, and shelter).

10. Refer the parents to community resources that can supplement income and/or food provision in order to ensure adequate nutrition for the family.

11. Assess the parents' expectations regarding adequate sleep patterns for the child. Include in the discussion the sleeping arrangements and bedtime environment.

12. Assess the parents' understanding of the requisites for and means of ensuring adequate sleep for the child.

13. Provide the parents with counseling on behavior management for implementing a reasonable sleep-wake schedule and routine for the child.

14. Assist the parents in identifying and correcting any aspects of the child's physical environment that might interfere with sleep.

15. Teach the parents about the need for the child to receive timely immunizations; discuss the potentially serious medical consequences of failure to immunize, and provide informational literature, if indicated.

16. Assist the parents in locating appropriate resources for immunizations for the child and in developing a plan for obtaining them.

17. Follow up to ensure that the child has received immunizations; redirect when necessary.

18. Determine whether the child is receiving routine medical check-ups and medical care when he/she is ill.

19. Assist the parents in locating appropriate resources for scheduling and receiving medical care; make appointments.

20. Monitor to ensure that the child receives routine medical care.

21. Assess the parents' understanding of the physical, emotional, and social needs of the child at the current developmental stage.

22. Provide the parents with educational information (e.g., pamphlets, books, Internet resources, and oral teaching) regarding the developmental needs of the child.

23. Assess the child for signs of deficits in physical, emotional, and/or social growth and development.

24. Assist the parents in identifying resources available to assist them in correcting the child's developmental deficits (e.g., pediatrician, dietitian, and child development specialist).

25. Monitor the parents' follow-through with interventions to correct the child's developmental deficits; assess the child's physical, emotional, and social environment to determine their adequacy to support the child's proper growth and development.

26. Assess the parents' knowledge of the symptoms of acute and chronic diseases in children.

27. Provide the parents with educational information

(e.g., books, pamphlets, Internet resources such as WebMD, and oral teaching) regarding the signs of acute or chronic diseases in children that require medical attention.

28. Direct the parents to medical resources in the event that the child shows signs of an acute or chronic illness.

29. Role-play scenarios with the parents of discovering signs that indicate the child needs medical attention and of taking the steps to obtain that attention.

___. _____
     _____

___. _____
     _____

___. _____
     _____

DIAGNOSTIC SUGGESTIONS

Axis I:	296.xx	Major Depressive Disorder
	311	Depressive Disorder NOS
	298.9	Psychotic Disorder NOS
	_____	_____
	_____	_____
Axis II:	V62.89	Borderline Intellectual Functioning
	317	Mild Mental Retardation
	318.0	Moderate Mental Retardation
	V71.09	No Diagnosis on Axis II
	799.9	Diagnosis Deferred on Axis II
	_____	_____
	_____	_____

NUTRITIONAL RISK/FOOD INSECURITY

BEHAVIORAL DEFINITIONS

1. Frequently lacks money to buy the necessary food to sustain healthy nutrition.
2. Eats alone most of the time.
3. Usually eats only one meal per day or does not eat a variety of foods from the major food groups.
4. Has experienced an involuntary loss or gain of 10 or more pounds in the last 6 months.
5. Is physically unable to shop or cook.
6. Consumes three or more drinks of beer, liquor, or wine almost daily.
7. Experiences frequent diarrhea, constipation, or dental problems.
8. Is a pregnant adult or teen and is not receiving prenatal care/counseling.
9. Is not self-sufficient in feeding or frequently loses food from the mouth, chokes on liquids or solids, or has difficulty sucking or chewing.
10. Has an illness or condition that requires a change in the kind and/or amount of food eaten.

__. _____
   _____
__. _____
   _____
__. _____
   _____

This chapter contributed by Lois Ann Wodarski.

LONG-TERM GOALS

1. Obtain emergency food relief and apply for long-term financial assistance.
2. Consume a daily diet that provides recommended nutrients and energy for physiological condition, age, and gender.
3. Obtain assistance as necessary for shopping for food, food preparation, and feeding.
4. Observe mealtimes that provide opportunities for social interaction and developmental skills building.
5. Obtain modified diets as needed for physical or psychological illness or condition (e.g., diabetes, pregnancy, or cerebral palsy).
6. Terminate alcohol and/or drug use that compromises nutritional status.
7. Obtain medical treatment for compromised health condition.

—. _____
_____
_____
—. _____
_____
_____
—. _____
_____

SHORT-TERM OBJECTIVES

1. Describe conditions of environment, eating habits, food sanitation, food preparation, and storage capabilities. (1, 2)
2. Verbalize the need for assistance in budgeting for food supplies, obtaining resources for food purchases, and food shopping or preparation. (3, 4, 5)
3. Follow through with a referral to a service agency or counselor to obtain nutritional assistance. (6)
4. Describe the adequacy of mealtime in meeting the

THERAPEUTIC INTERVENTIONS

1. Observe the client's physical environment or interview the client to determine the adequacy of his/her food supply and food sanitation, preparation, and storage capabilities.

2. Assess the client's daily food intake patterns, food preparation and storage techniques, and adequacy of resources for food purchases, preparation, and storage.

3. Refer the client for emergency food relief from private or government

family member's social as well as nutritional needs. (7, 8)

5. Verbalize difficulties in mealtime behavior, self-feeding, dietary intake, or opportunities for mealtime social interaction. (8, 9, 10)

6. Identify how dietary interventions that have been prescribed for nutritional problems are now being implemented. (10, 11)

7. Describe the adequacy of the prescribed regimen in controlling or resolving nutritional problems. (11, 12)

8. Describe alcohol consumption patterns and/or medication and drug use that may interfere with intake, digestion, or absorption of nutrients. (13)

9. Agree to screening for alcohol or drug abuse. (13, 14)

10. Cooperate with an evaluation by a physician of prescription drug interaction with appetite, absorption of nutrients, or other nutritional deficits. (13, 15)

__. _____
   _____
__. _____
   _____
__. _____
   _____

community resources and facilitate his/her obtaining assistance.

4. If daily food intake appears insufficient or omits major categories of foods (e.g., milk or milk products or protein foods [meats, beans, and grains]) refer the client to a local Women, Infants, and Children's (WIC) program, Office on Aging, county health department, family independence agency, senior center, or early intervention program as appropriate for long-term assistance.

5. If deficiencies in food budgeting, preparation, or storage are noted, refer the client to a local WIC program, Office on Aging, county health department, or county extension service, as appropriate.

6. Monitor and reinforce the client's follow-through on obtaining community services to relieve his/her nutritional crisis.

7. Observe the client or ask him/her to describe the mealtime social and parental interactions (especially if the client is a dependent infant, child, or adult) in order to determine whether proper attention is given to all family members' nutritional needs.

8. Determine the appropriateness of the mealtime situation in developing or reinforcing social or developmental skills.

9. If problems in self-feeding are noted, assess the need for a medical evaluation, occupational or physical therapy consultation, or adaptive equipment.

10. Refer the client to a registered dietician, occupational therapist, or physical therapist if prescriptions for such services are not in effect.

11. Monitor and reinforce the client's effective implementation of the prescribed nutritional interventions.

12. Assess the adequacy of the prescribed regimen in resolving the client's nutritional problems.

13. Explore the client's alcohol intake and drug or medication use regarding its possible impact on nutrition (e.g., intake and absorption).

14. If the client's alcohol intake exceeds three drinks per day, of if there is evidence of street drug use, refer him/her for an alcohol and drug use risk evaluation.

15. Refer the client to a physician who can evaluate the impact of the client's prescription medications on his/her nutritional deficits.

__. _____

_____

__. _____

_____

__. _____

_____

DIAGNOSTIC SUGGESTIONS

Axis I:

309.0	Adjustment Disorder With Depressed Mood
309.24	Adjustment Disorder With Anxiety
309.28	Adjustment Disorder With Mixed Anxiety and Depressed Mood
296.xx	Major Depressive Disorder
300.00	Anxiety Disorder NOS
V62.2	Occupational Problem
295.30	Schizophrenia, Paranoid Type
295.10	Schizophrenia, Disorganized Type
295.90	Schizophrenia, Undifferentiated Type
298.9	Psychotic Disorder NOS
296.xx	Bipolar I Disorder
296.80	Bipolar Disorder NOS
——	————————
——	————————

Axis II:

301.0	Paranoid Personality Disorder
301.20	Schizoid Personality Disorder
301.22	Schizotypal Personality Disorder
V71.09	No Diagnosis on Axis II
799.9	Diagnosis Deferred on Axis II
——	————————
——	————————

OLDER ADULT ABUSE

BEHAVIORAL DEFINITIONS

1. Self-report of verbal, physical, sexual, or financial abuse.
2. Reports by family, neighbors, friends or police that the patient has been a victim of verbal, physical, sexual, or financial abuse.
3. Self-report of medication, personal aids, clothing, or food being withheld by others.
4. Evidence of physical or sexual abuse: bruises; bone fractures; red, swollen, or torn genitalia; or open sores.
5. Evidence of being forced to leave home and unnecessarily enter an institutional setting.
6. Lack of access to financial assets due to undesired outside control from others.
7. Deterioration in physical health due to food, medical care, and/or medication being withheld.
8. Depressed affect, low energy, sleep disturbances, and tearful spells.
9. Fearful isolation and withdrawal in an attempt to protect self from anticipated future abuse.

—. _____
   _____
—. _____
   _____
—. _____
   _____

LONG TERM GOALS

1. Terminate verbal, physical, sexual, or financial abuse.

2. Live in a safe environment with freedom to make own decisions without fear of reprisal.
3. Regain control over own finances.
4. Develop a trusting relationship with a person who will control finances in client's best interest.
5. Overcome depression and return to a sense of joy, peace, and security.
6. Gain access to nutritious meals on a daily basis.
7. Regain health, physical strength, and social freedom.

—. _____

_____

—. _____

_____

—. _____

_____

SHORT-TERM OBJECTIVES

1. Describe the details regarding the nature, extent, frequency, and perpetrator of abuse. (1, 2, 3)
2. Participate in a medical examination to assess consequences of physical and/or nutrition abuse. (4, 5, 6)
3. Obtain ongoing recommended medical care. (6)
4. Cooperate with a psychological and/or neuropsychological evaluation to assess consequences of the emotional, sexual, physical, or verbal abuse. (5, 7, 8)
5. Accept referral to counseling to heal emotional scars resulting from abuse. (8, 9)
6. Verbalize feelings of fear, intimidation, or shame associated with the abuse. (10, 11)

THERAPEUTIC INTERVENTIONS

1. Build rapport with the client through consistent eye contact, unconditional positive regard, warm acceptance, soft voice, conversation about nonthreatening topics, and expressions of reassurance regarding the client's safety.
2. Slowly explore the details of the client's abuse without pressing the client beyond his/her level of trust.
3. Change the subject to less threatening topics before gently returning for more open probing of the facts of the abuse.
4. Refer the client to a physician for examination of the consequences of the abuse.

7. Describe any fears regarding the perpetrator seeking revenge for being reported. (12)

8. Agree to and then make contact with legal authorities to seek protection for self. (13, 14)

9. Agree to testify in court against perpetrator of the abuse. (15, 16)

10. Verbalize agreement that responsibility for the abuse falls on the perpetrator, not on self. (17, 18, 19)

11. Verbalize feelings toward the perpetrator of the abuse. (19, 20)

12. Describe nutritional needs and desires that have not been met and the means others took to deprive self of these essentials. (21, 22)

13. Return to eating nutritional meals on a regular basis. (22, 23, 24)

14. List financial assets and describe how control has been lost over these assets. (25, 26)

15. Select someone who can be trusted to help oversee finances. (27, 28, 29)

16. Make social contacts freely and with increased frequency. (30, 31)

17. Describe options for a safer living environment. (32)

18. Move to a safer environment where rights will be respected. (32, 33, 34, 35)

5. Obtain a written confidentiality release from the client to allow for contact with the evaluating professional in order to share information regarding the abuse and to obtain the results and recommendations of the evaluation.

6. Facilitate and monitor the client's access to more medical services as recommended by the examining physician.

7. Refer the client for a psychological and/or neuropsychological evaluation to assess the emotional and/or cognitive consequences of the abuse.

8. Coordinate the client's obtaining ongoing treatment for psychological problems resulting from the abuse; refer the client to an appropriate counseling provider.

9. Monitor and reinforce the client's follow-through on obtaining necessary counseling services.

10. Explore the client's emotional reaction to the abuse, allowing for a free expression of feelings in an accepting atmosphere of support.

11. Suggest that the client write a journal of feelings that occur on a daily basis and then bring written material to future counseling sessions for sharing.

19. Report reduced feelings of stress, fear, and shame. (36, 37)

20. Become active in community-based elderly support groups to build self-esteem, social activity, and resources for assistance. (38)

21. Agree to regularly scheduled telephone and/or visitation contact by a caseworker. (38, 39, 40)

—. _____
    _____

—. _____
    _____

—. _____
    _____

12. Assess the client's safety from retaliation by the perpetrator of the abuse.

13. Encourage the client to make contact with legal authorities to obtain protection from further abuse; accompany the client in making this contact, if necessary.

14. Monitor the client's ongoing safety for any incidents or threats of further abuse.

15. Encourage and empower the client to assert his/her right to protection from the law by testifying against the perpetrator of the abuse.

16. Provide emotional and moral support to the client as he/she follows through with legal testimony against the perpetrator of the abuse.

17. Confront the client for excusing the perpetrator and reinforce all statements that place clear responsibility on the perpetrator for the abuse.

18. Provide a more reality-based view of circumstances of the abuse as the client tends to take on blame for the abuse or excuse the perpetrator's actions.

19. Structure an empty chair exercise in which the client tells the perpetrator what the perpetrator has done, why it is wrong, and how the client feels about it.

20. Explore the future of the client's relationship with the perpetrator of the abuse, especially if the perpetrator is a family member or "friend."

21. Explore facts and the client's feelings related to deprivation of his/her nutritional needs and desires.

22. Refer the client for nutritional assessment and education.

23. Establish and monitor the client's meal routine.

24. Explore the client's options for meal opportunities provided by community agencies.

25. Encourage the client to develop a list of his/her financial assets.

26. Assist the client in examining the chain of events that led to the loss of control of his/her assets.

27. Assist the client in problem solving how to protect his/her assets.

28. Explore options of trusted persons who would help to oversee the client's finances.

29. Refer the client to an attorney to establish a conservatorship, if necessary.

30. Explore with the client opportunities for increased social contacts with family and friends and participation in community activities.

31. Encourage and monitor the client's social contacts and

participation in social activities.

32. Assist the client in identifying safe alternative living arrangements.

33. Assist the client in selecting a safer living environment.

34. Explore the client's feelings related to the decision to move to a safer environment.

35. Provide the client with emotional support through the housing transition.

36. Teach the client stress-management and relaxation techniques.

37. Reframe the client's perspective to place all the responsibility for the abuse on the perpetrator.

38. Link the client to available community supports and resources (e.g., Meals on Wheels, Office on Aging, or local senior center).

39. Suggest that the client accept case-management services as available.

40. Monitor to ensure that the linkages between the client and the community resources are made.

___. _____

_____

___. _____

_____

___. _____

_____

DIAGNOSTIC SUGGESTIONS

Axis I:	309.0	Adjustment Disorder With Depressed Mood
	309.24	Adjustment Disorder With Anxiety
	296.2x	Major Depressive Disorder, Single Episode
	300.02	Generalized Anxiety Disorder
	995.81	Sexual Abuse of Adult (Victim)
	308.3	Acute Stress Disorder
	309.81	Posttraumatic Stress Disorder
	_____	_____
	_____	_____
Axis II:	301.82	Avoidant Personality Disorder
	301.6	Dependent Personality Disorder
	_____	_____
	_____	_____

OLDER ADULT ISOLATION

BEHAVIORAL DEFINITIONS

1. Feelings of loneliness and depression related to losses associated with aging.
2. Lack of satisfying social interactions and activities.
3. Lack of social support system of friends.
4. Little or no family support and/or contact.
5. Decreased mobility and strength necessary to get out of the home due to decline in physical health.
6. Inhibited ability to participate in social activities due to inadequate finances.
7. Lack of transportation to allow independence and participation in activities.
8. Fear of leaving the safety of the home due to feelings of vulnerability.

__. _____
   _____
__. _____
   _____
__. _____
   _____

LONG-TERM GOALS

1. Overcome depression and return to a sense of joy and peace.
2. Acquire meaningful social interactions.
3. Develop a social support system.
4. Increase family contact and support.

5. Regain health and physical strength to allow social freedom.
6. Participate in social activities that do not require financial support.
7. Utilize alternate transportation resources to increase social contacts.
8. Develop a social network despite physical limitations.

—. _____
_____
_____

—. _____
_____
_____

—. _____
_____

SHORT-TERM OBJECTIVES

1. Cooperate with an assessment of current cognitive, social, and emotional functioning. (1, 2)
2. Accept referral for psychiatric evaluation. (2, 3)
3. Take antidepressant medication as prescribed. (4, 5, 6)
4. Report as to the effectiveness of psychotropic medication in decreasing depressive symptoms. (4, 5, 6, 7)
5. Describe feelings of loss related to aging and isolation. (1, 8, 9)
6. Identify barriers to socialization and means to overcome them. (1, 9, 29)
7. Participate in a medical examination to assess physical health and mobility. (10)

THERAPEUTIC INTERVENTIONS

1. Build rapport with the client through consistent eye contact, unconditional positive regard, warm acceptance, and soft voice.
2. Assess the client's cognitive and emotional functioning as well as the need for a psychiatric evaluation.
3. Refer the client for psychiatric evaluation that will include assessment for antidepressant medication.
4. Educate the client in regard to the medication's expected effectiveness, side effects, and the importance of consistent adherence to the prescribed dosage.
5. Explain to the client the importance of self-monitoring the medication's effectiveness and reporting back to the professional.

8. Comply with the physician's recommendations for improving physical functioning. (11)

9. Family members cooperate with the psychosocial assessment process. (12, 13)

10. Family members verbalize increased understanding of the client's isolation, medication regimen, and need for increased family interaction. (14, 15)

11. Family members and the client increase the frequency of social contact. (15, 16, 17, 18)

12. Identify social support programs in the community that would be enjoyable and meet the need for socialization. (19, 20)

13. Accept referral to appropriate community programs for older adults. (21, 22)

14. Become active in community-based elderly support groups to build self-esteem, social activity, and resources for assistance. (22, 23)

15. Accept referral to financial assistance programs in the community. (24, 25)

16. Identify transportation options in the community. (26, 27)

17. Agree to regularly scheduled telephone and/or visitation contact by a caseworker. (28)

18. Discuss fears related to leaving the home. (9, 29)

6. Reinforce the client for consistently taking medications.

7. Monitor and assess the client's medication for effectiveness and side effects; communicate results to the prescribing physician.

8. Explore the client's feelings of grief and loss related to aging.

9. Explore the client's perception as to why he/she has become more isolated (e.g., health, transportation, fear, finances, or death of friends); process ways to overcome these barriers to socializations.

10. Refer the client for a medical examination.

11. Encourage the client to follow the physician's recommendations; facilitate the client's follow-through with necessary tests and treatments.

12. Obtain psychosocial information from the client's family members, focusing on their history of availability and motivation for involvement with the client.

13. Assess the family support system and encourage the family members' involvement in the client's life to the extent the client desires.

14. Educate the involved family members as to the client's isolation and medication regime.

19. Report a reduction in fear of leaving home to reduce isolation. (30, 31)

—. _____
   _____
—. _____
   _____
—. _____
   _____

15. Encourage and reinforce the client's and family members' interaction.

16. Develop a schedule of regular family contact with the client that is agreeable to everyone.

17. Develop a telephone contact schedule between the client and the family members.

18. Assist the family members and the client in developing a list of activities within the client's physical and financial limitations that they can enjoy together.

19. Assess the client's current community support system needs.

20. Review with the client all available community resources that could provide socialization opportunities.

21. Obtain a written confidentiality release from the client to allow for contact with community programs in order to facilitate referrals.

22. Link the client with community programming (e.g., Office on Aging, or local senior center, church, and case-management services).

23. Monitor and reinforce the client's attendance at community-based support programs.

24. Assess the client's financial situation and eligibility for public assistance.

25. Link the client with financial assistance programs

(e.g., food stamps, food pantries, and Supplementary Security Income).

26. Assess the client's resources for transportation (e.g., own vehicle, family, bus, cab, or friends).

27. Link the client to transportation alternatives in the community (e.g., public transportation, Medicaid transporter, Office on Aging, or volunteers).

28. Monitor the client to ensure that the linkages to the community resources are made and maintained.

29. Explore the client's fear of leaving home as to its origins in real or imagined experience.

30. Brainstorm with the client what measures could be taken to decrease the client's fear and increase his/her sense of security (e.g., accompaniment by a friend or family member, increased police presence in the community, or formation of a neighborhood watch).

31. Challenge the client's unrealistic, imagined fears and reassure the client as to his/her relative safety.

__. _____
    _____

__. _____
    _____

__. _____
    _____

DIAGNOSTIC SUGGESTIONS

Axis I: 309.0   Adjustment Disorder With Depressed Mood
                296.2x   Major Depressive Disorder, Single Episode

                _____   _____

                _____   _____

Axis II: 301.82   Avoidant Personality Disorder

                _____   _____

                _____   _____

OLDER ADULT RESIDENTIAL ADJUSTMENT

BEHAVIORAL DEFINITIONS

1. Need for a long-term, supervised, residential setting due to decline in cognitive and/or physical abilities.
2. Grief related to separation from family and friends.
3. Grief related to loss of home and belongings.
4. Feelings of depression, isolation, and loneliness.
5. Multiple health issues.
6. Decline in ability to function independently.

__. _____
   _____
__. _____
   _____
__. _____
   _____

LONG-TERM GOALS

1. Adjust to the supervised residential setting.
2. Obtain adequate family and social support.
3. Decrease feelings of depression, isolation, and loneliness.
4. Obtain necessary medical or psychiatric care.
5. Optimize independent functioning within the supervised setting.

—. _____
  _____
  _____

—. _____
  _____
  _____

—. _____
  _____
  _____

SHORT-TERM OBJECTIVES	THERAPEUTIC INTERVENTIONS
1. Report a feeling of acclimation to new surroundings. (1, 2, 3)	1. Provide the client and the family members with facility information, a tour of the facility, and an introduction to the staff.
2. Participate in the admission process and provide necessary information and signatures. (4)	
3. Family members participate in the admission process and provide necessary information. (1, 4, 5)	2. Provide the client with copies of the residents' bill of rights, facility rules and regulations, and available services and activities.
4. Maintain contact with family and friends. (5, 6)	3. Provide information on personal telephone service in the client's room and facilitate the service if requested.
5. Participate in the development of a treatment plan. (4, 7, 8)	
6. Participate in planned activities in the facility. (9, 10)	4. Gather psychosocial information from the client and available family members.
7. Socialize with other residents. (10, 11)	5. Inform family members and friends of visiting hours and regulations.
8. Demonstrate current cognitive, social, and emotional functioning in a mental status exam. (12)	6. Encourage a time of first visitation for family and friends of the client to set a precedent and to reduce fear of abandonment.
9. Cooperate with a referral for a psychiatric evaluation. (4, 12, 13)	7. Encourage the client to actively participate in formulating the initial treatment plan.
10. Verbalize an understanding of the necessity for taking	

psychotropic medications and agree to cooperate with prescribed care. (14)

11. Take medications as prescribed and report as to their effectiveness and side effects. (15, 16)

12. Report a decrease in anxiety and/or depressive symptoms. (16)

13. Cooperate with a required physical exam. (17)

14. Comply with the physician's recommendations and treatment. (18)

15. Accept referrals for ancillary services. (19, 20)

16. Perform the optimal level of self-care as physically capable. (19, 20, 21)

17. Participate in quarterly treatment plan reviews. (22, 23, 24)

—. _____
_____
—. _____
_____
—. _____
_____

8. Provide the client with opportunities to verbalize his/her goals in the treatment-planning process.

9. Educate the client regarding activities available in the facility and provide a written calendar of events.

10. Introduce the client to his/her peers and encourage socialization.

11. Monitor the client's social contact with peers, encouraging and reinforcing socialization.

12. Complete a mental status exam to rule out clinical depression and/or anxiety.

13. Refer the client for a psychiatric evaluation and medication.

14. Educate the client regarding the medication's expected effectiveness and side effects, as well as the importance of consistent adherence to the medication regime.

15. Monitor and reinforce the client's compliance in consistently taking prescribed psychotropic medications.

16. Assess the client's psychotropic medication for effectiveness and side effects; communicate results to the prescribing physician.

17. Refer the client for a physical examination.

18. Monitor and reinforce the client's compliance with the physician's treatment and recommendations.

19. Refer the client for ancillary services (e.g., activity, occupational, and physical therapy).

20. Educate the client as to the benefits associated with accepting and participating in ancillary services.

21. Encourage mobility and independence within the client's ability (e.g., self-care, eating meals in the community dining room, walking).

22. Invite the client to each treatment plan review and encourage his/her attendance and active participation.

23. Encourage the client to voice complaints, desires, and ideas in treatment-planning meetings.

24. Monitor the client's adjustment to the new residential setting.

__. _____
    _____

__. _____
    _____

__. _____
    _____

DIAGNOSTIC SUGGESTIONS

Axis I:	309.0	Adjustment Disorder With Depressed Mood
	309.24	Adjustment Disorder With Anxiety
	309.28	Adjustment Disorder With Anxiety and Depressed Mood
	_____	_____
	_____	_____

PARTNER ABUSE

BEHAVIORAL DEFINITIONS

1. Hitting, punching, or kicking an adult family member.
2. Using weapons or instruments to hurt an adult family member.
3. Forcing an adult family member to engage in sexual acts.
4. Shoving, pushing, or scratching an adult family member.
5. Threatening an adult family member.
6. Insulting or shaming an adult family member in front of others.
7. Belittling or ridiculing an adult family member.
8. Behaving in a manner that causes police to be called to the home in response to domestic violence.

—. _____

_____

—. _____

_____

—. _____

_____

LONG-TERM GOALS

1. Eliminate verbal and/or physical abuse.
2. Participate in conjoint, individual, and/or group counseling focused on domestic violence.
3. Reduce stress in the home environment.
4. Increase marital (common law) satisfaction of each of the partners.
5. Increase the positive self-images of the marital (common law) partners.
6. Increase conflict-resolution skills of all family members.

—. _____
   _____
   _____

—. _____
   _____
   _____

—. _____
   _____
   _____

SHORT-TERM OBJECTIVES

1. Describe the history and nature of abuse. (1, 2)

2. Describe the conditions of the home environment. (2)

3. Verbalize an understanding of the need to be moved to a safer environment. (3)

4. The client and the perpetrator accept the need for a separation. (3, 4)

5. Verbalize the need to be self-supporting. (5)

6. Partners agree to conditions for remaining together. (6)

7. Perpetrator agrees to rules for safe interaction with the partner. (6, 7)

8. Pledge in front of the perpetrator to contact police if violence threatens to erupt in the future. (8, 9)

9. Partners list the triggers that escalate violence and safe responses to those triggers. (10)

10. Partners accept and follow through on a referral to a group treatment focused on relationship skills training. (11, 18)

THERAPEUTIC INTERVENTIONS

1. Interview both partners separately as to the nature and history of abuse (i.e., verbal and/or physical; specify frequency and intensity).

2. Observe and evaluate the current physical and emotional environment of the home; review any available case histories for descriptions of the environment. Determine whether the client and partner can live in safety together.

3. If an immediate physical threat exists, locate the client and refer him/her to an appropriate shelter in order to provide a safe environment for the client and any children. Assist in relocation.

4. If it is determined that the partners cannot live safely together, recommend and facilitate separation.

5. Assess the client's ability to be self-supporting in terms of financial and psychosocial resources. If the

11. Perpetrator accepts and follows through on a referral to an anger-management group. (12, 18)

12. Perpetrator attends a domestic violence treatment group. (13, 14, 18)

13. Attend an assertiveness training group. (9, 15, 16, 18)

14. Partners attend marital counseling. (17, 18)

15. List the external sources of stress that raise the tension level within the relationship. (19, 20)

16. Each partner describes his/her history and patterns of alcohol and drug use. (21)

17. Terminate substance abuse and attend treatment on a consistent basis. (18, 21, 22, 23)

—. _____
   _____
—. _____
   _____
—. _____
   _____

client is employable, refer him/her for vocational counseling. If the client is not employable, secure subsidized living arrangements and child care, if necessary.

6. Assist the client in developing a decision matrix for remaining in the relationship (e.g., what boundaries must be maintained, what changes must be made to promote safety, and what legal sanctions will occur if violence erupts).

7. If it is determined that the partners can remain together, outline the rules for interaction (e.g., no threats, insults, physical assaults, hitting, or weapons); solicit the perpetrator's clear agreement with these rules.

8. Establish a safety procedure for the client if violence is threatened in the future; solicit the client's pledge to enact the procedure before violence erupts.

9. Affirm and reinforce the client's right to respectful, safe treatment even when the perpetrator's anger is triggered.

10. Teach the partners to recognize and list the escalating triggers for verbal and physical abuse and violence; role-play escape or deescalating responses to these triggers.

11. Refer the partners to a relationship skills training group.

12. Refer the perpetrator to treatment for anger management.

13. Refer the perpetrator to a domestic violence treatment group.

14. Contact court authorities regarding making the perpetrator's attendance at treatment a compulsory part of sentencing or probation.

15. Teach the partners the distinction between passivity, assertiveness, and aggression.

16. Refer the client to an assertiveness training group.

17. Refer the partners to a community agency that provides marital counseling.

18. Monitor and reinforce follow-through with recommendations regarding psychological and relationship treatment; process and eliminate any barriers to access to mental health services.

19. Assist the partners in identifying the external stressors (e.g., lack of employment, indebtedness, extended family issues, illness, or disability).

20. Explore with the partners adaptive responses that could reduce external sources of stress; refer them to appropriate agencies for

support (e.g., medical care, disability income, or care for aging).

21. Explore and assess the history, amount, nature, and frequency of the partners' substance abuse.

22. Assess the role of substance abuse in the domestic violence; refer for in-depth chemical dependence evaluation and treatment.

23. Refer the substance-abusing partner to Alcoholics Anonymous (AA) and the client to Alanon meetings.

__. _____

    _____

__. _____

    _____

__. _____

    _____

DIAGNOSTIC SUGGESTIONS

Axis I:	V71.01	Adult Antisocial Behavior
	296.xx	Bipolar I Disorder
	296.89	Bipolar II Disorder
	312.34	Intermittent Explosive Disorder
	___	_____
	___	_____
Axis II:	301.7	Antisocial Personality Disorder
	301.0	Paranoid Personality Disorder
	301.9	Personality Disorder NOS
	V71.09	No Diagnosis on Axis II
	799.9	Diagnosis Deferred on Axis II
	___	_____
	___	_____

PHYSICAL/COGNITIVE DISABILITY

BEHAVIORAL DEFINITIONS

1. A diagnosed serious medical condition that needs attention and has an impact on daily living (e.g., high blood pressure, asthma, seizures, diabetes, heart disease, cancer, or cirrhosis).
2. Constant chronic pain that is debilitating and depressing.
3. A medical condition for which the client is under a physician's care.
4. Cognitive confusion and/or memory loss that interferes with the ability to perform activities of daily living.
5. Physical disability that limits freedom of movement and choice of activity.
6. Developmental disability that leads to a need for specialized medical, psychological, educational, and/or vocational training services.
7. Illness and/or aging complications that contribute to weakness, frailty, and need for supportive services.
8. Lack of follow through on medical treatment regimen.
9. Behavioral patterns and/or environmental stressors that exacerbate or complicate a medical condition.
10. Lack of necessary social support systems to reduce the effects of disease (e.g., extended family, friendships, self-help groups, or support groups).

__. _____
   _____
__. _____
   _____
__. _____
   _____

LONG-TERM GOALS

1. Follow through with necessary medical treatment for physical malady.
2. Access medical or psychological care available from community resources.
3. Medically stabilize physical condition.
4. Access and implement pain-management procedures.
5. Family supports member who has an illness, injury, and/or cognitive deficit.
6. Access services that will ameliorate the development disability.
7. Access services and develop coping skills to compensate for cognitive deficits.

__. _____

_____

__. _____

_____

__. _____

_____

SHORT-TERM OBJECTIVES

1. Describe the history, nature, and treatment of the current medical condition or physical/cognitive disability. (1, 2)
2. Verbalize an awareness of the community- and government-supported medical services available. (3, 4)
3. Apply for medical insurance or government-subsidized medical services. (3, 4)
4. Comply totally with doctor's orders for tests, medications, limitations, and/or treatments. (5, 6)

THERAPEUTIC INTERVENTIONS

1. Gather a history of the client's medical condition or physical/cognitive disability.
2. Assess the urgency of the client's need for medical care and take immediate action to obtain access to medical services, if necessary.
3. Teach the client and family about community- and government-supported medical insurance and services that the client is eligible for.
4. Refer the client and family to the proper social services agency to apply for

5. Cooperate fully with ongoing prescribed medical treatment regimen. (5, 6, 7, 8)

6. Accept the need for an assisted living environment due to physical and/or cognitive deficits. (9, 10, 11)

7. Move into a supervised, assisted living environment. (10, 12)

8. Terminate denial and accept the need for assistance. (1, 2, 5, 13)

9. Apply for and accept financial aid. (4, 14)

10. Participate in an assessment and training program for the developmentally disabled. (11, 15, 16)

11. Describe use of mood-altering substances, nicotine, caffeine, and unbalanced diet that could contribute to medical deterioration. (17)

12. Implement positive, health-related behaviors that enhance the quality of life, such as reducing caffeine intake, ceasing to smoke, balancing diet, patterning the sleep/wake cycle, and terminating substance abuse. (18, 19)

13. Family members verbalize an acceptance of the client's physical or mental limitations and demonstrate support for the client's rehabilitation. (7, 20, 21, 22)

14. Modify the living environment and/or lifestyle to re-

government-subsidized medical insurance (e.g., Medicare or Medicaid).

5. Monitor the client's follow-through and success with obtaining necessary medical care; redirect when necessary.

6. Facilitate the client's obtaining medical treatment (e.g., make appointment and arrange transportation).

7. Reinforce the family members' support of the client's follow-through with the treatment regimen.

8. Help the client understand his/her medical problem and the need to cooperate with the doctor's recommendations.

9. Assess the client's need for a more supervised assisted-living environment (e.g., frailty, confusion, or cognitive deficits).

10. Refer the client for an evaluation at an assisted-living facility; facilitate the appointment.

11. Refer the client for a psychological and mental status assessment of cognitive limitations.

12. Facilitate the client's admission to a facility that will provide assisted-living services.

13. Assess the client's denial of the seriousness of his/her condition; confront denial

duce stress and improve health. (23, 24)

15. Identify sources of social and emotional support and increase the frequency of these contacts. (25, 26)

__. _____

_____

__. _____

_____

__. _____

_____

and present reality-based facts that require attention.

14. Direct the client and family to social services resources that can provide financial aid.

15. Refer the client for an educational or vocational assessment with respect to his/her developmental disability.

16. Facilitate and monitor the client's admission into a program to address his/her developmental disability.

17. Explore and assess the client's substance abuse and other unhealthy living patterns that exacerbate his/her medical decline.

18. Refer the client for an in-depth substance abuse evaluation and possible treatment.

19. Recommend a reduction or elimination of the consumption of unhealthy foods, nicotine, and high amounts of caffeine, as well as the implementation of adequate sleep and exercise.

20. Explain the client's disability to the family members and list steps they can take to show support.

21. Refer the family members to a support group of others struggling with a similar adjustment.

22. Encourage and support the family members as they disclose their fears, frustra-

tions, and concerns regarding the client's adjustment.

23. Assess the client's and family members' social and physical environment in regard to preventive health (e.g., safety, nutrition, and sanitation knowledge and practices).

24. Explore for external factors that increase stress (e.g., employment, finances, interpersonal conflict, and isolation); develop coping mechanisms or remedial actions that can alleviate stress.

25. Explore with the client and family members potential sources of social support (e.g., extended family, self-help groups, or support groups).

26. Facilitate the client's and family members' utilization of appropriate social support mechanisms.

—. _____

_____

—. _____

_____

—. _____

_____

DIAGNOSTIC SUGGESTIONS

Axis I:	309.0	Adjustment Disorder With Depressed Mood
	309.24	Adjustment Disorder With Anxiety
	309.28	Adjustment Disorder With Mixed Anxiety and Depressed Mood

780.9	Age-Related Cognitive Decline
307.80	Pain Disorder Associated With Psychological Factors
307.89	Pain Disorder Associated With Both Psychological Factors and a General Medical Condition
316	Maladaptive Health Behaviors Affecting General Medical Condition
316	Stress-Related Physiological Response Affecting General Medical Condition
294.8	Amnestic Disorder NOS
294.9	Cognitive Disorder NOS
294.1	Dementia Due to General Medical Condition
300.00	Anxiety Disorder NOS
——	———————————
——	———————————

Axis II:

V71.09	No Diagnosis on Axis II
799.9	Diagnosis Deferred on Axis II
——	———————————
——	———————————

POVERTY

BEHAVIORAL DEFINITIONS

1. Inadequate financial income.
2. Inadequate food and nutrition.
3. Lack of medical and dental care.
4. Lack of appropriate clothing.
5. Substandard housing or lack of housing.
6. Lack of transportation.
7. Stress related to living in poverty.
8. Lack of opportunity to advance self.
9. Lack of job skills or experience with job interviewing.
10. Social maladjustment related to chronic mental illness.
11. Financial and employment deficits related to chronic medical disability.

—. _____
   _____
—. _____
   _____
—. _____
   _____

LONG-TERM GOALS

1. Obtain emergency financial assistance necessary for obtaining food and shelter.
2. Gain access to adequate food and nutrition.
3. Obtain access to medical treatment and preventive care.
4. Obtain weather-appropriate clothing.
5. Obtain safe, clean, warm housing.

6. Gain access to transportation as needed.
7. Obtain treatment for medical and/or psychiatric conditions.
8. Participate in vocational assessment and job search skills training.
9. Obtain employment that will provide income above poverty level.

—. _____
   _____
   _____

—. _____
   _____
   _____

—. _____
   _____

SHORT-TERM OBJECTIVES

1. Describe current level and sources of income and methods of housing, food, and clothing procurement. (1, 2)

2. Identify factors contributing to poverty and ways to overcome barriers. (3, 4)

3. Identify feelings of stress, fear, and shame related to living in poverty. (5)

4. Cooperate with a mental status examination to assess for psychopathology. (6)

5. Obtain the recommended mental health services. (7, 8)

6. Apply for short-term emergency financial assistance. (9, 10)

7. Apply for long-term financial assistance through government-supported programs. (10, 11)

8. Express a desire for obtaining work. (12, 13, 14, 15)

THERAPEUTIC INTERVENTIONS

1. Build rapport with the client through consistent eye contact, unconditional positive regard, and warm acceptance.

2. Explore the client's history of poverty and current financial condition.

3. Assist the client in identifying the factors contributing to his/her poverty.

4. Teach the client problem-solving skills as applied to the factors causing his/her poverty.

5. Explore the client's feelings related to his/her current financial and living situation.

6. Assess the client's mental status to determine if a referral for a more in-depth psychological evaluation is indicated.

7. Refer for a more in-depth psychological or psychiatric

9. Utilize community-based food programs. (16, 17)

10. Access government-subsidized medical and dental services. (18, 19, 20)

11. Obtain and maintain adequate weather-appropriate clothing. (21, 22, 23)

12. Utilize emergency shelter housing on a temporary basis. (24)

13. Apply for government-subsidized permanent housing. (25)

14. Contact the authorities regarding violations of housing code by landlord. (26)

15. Identify transportation resources. (27)

16. Identify ways to improve educational and/or vocational skills. (28)

—. _____
   _____

—. _____
   _____

—. _____
   _____

evaluation to determine whether treatment is needed.

8. Facilitate the client's follow-through with any recommendations for mental health treatment (e.g., locate appropriate community services and facilitate transportation and financial assistance).

9. Refer the client to public financial assistance programs to determine eligibility for an immediate stipend.

10. Teach the client about the government programs available for long-term financial assistance and determine the client's possible eligibility for these programs.

11. Refer the client for Supplemental Security Income, Social Security Disability, or worker's compensation as appropriate.

12. Assess the client's ability and motivation to work.

13. Assist the client in identifying employment opportunities.

14. Refer the client for a vocational assessment.

15. Link the client to employment services such as job search or job skills training.

16. Refer the client for food stamps, free school lunch program, and the Women, Infants, and Children (WIC) program as appropriate.

17. Link the client to area food pantries and soup kitchens.

18. Refer the client for Medicaid.

19. Provide the client with a list of free medical and dental clinics in the area.

20. Link the client to the local health department for available services.

21. Link the client to local non-profit agencies that provide clothing assistance.

22. Refer the client for emergency clothing money through public assistance.

23. Problem-solve with the client how clothing will be cleaned on a regular basis.

24. Link the client to emergency housing or shelter if needed.

25. Refer the client to a Housing and Urban Development office to complete an application for subsidized housing.

26. Refer the client to a government office for housing code enforcement if the current landlord is not maintaining the property in accordance with the law.

27. Brainstorm with the client regarding transportation options in the community.

28. Urge and empower the client to advance himself/herself through further vocational training or education.

—. _____

_____

—. _____

_____

—. _____

_____

DIAGNOSTIC SUGGESTIONS

Axis I: 309.0   Adjustment Disorder With Depressed Mood
309.24   Adjustment Disorder With Anxiety
309.28   Adjustment Disorder With Mixed Anxiety and
Depressed Mood
296.xx   Major Depressive Disorder
300.00   Anxiety Disorder NOS
V62.2   Occupational Problem
295.30   Schizophrenia, Paranoid Type
295.10   Schizophrenia, Disorganized Type
295.90   Schizophrenia, Undifferentiated Type
298.9   Psychotic Disorder NOS
296.xx   Bipolar I Disorder
296.80   Bipolar Disorder NOS

_____   _____

_____   _____

Axis II: 301.0   Paranoid Personality Disorder
301.20   Schizoid Personality Disorder
301.22   Schizotypal Personality Disorder
V71.09   No Diagnosis on Axis II
799.9   Diagnosis Deferred on Axis II

_____   _____

_____   _____

PROSTITUTION

BEHAVIORAL DEFINITIONS

1. Engages in prostitution as a means of financial support.
2. Engages in prostitution to support a habit of alcohol and/or drug dependence.
3. Allows self to be used sexually in exchange for food, shelter, and/or drugs.
4. Lacks adequate economic support.
5. Lacks employment skills.
6. Engages in theft or other dangerous activities to obtain income.
7. Feels lonely, depressed, and afraid.

—. _____
   _____
—. _____
   _____
—. _____
   _____

LONG-TERM GOALS

1. Terminate prostitution.
2. Obtain adequate safe housing, health care, and food access.
3. Obtain legal employment.
4. Acknowledge chemical dependence and participate in a treatment program for abstinence and recovery.
5. Overcome depression and anxiety and return to a sense of joy, peace, and security.

—. _____
   _____
   _____

—. _____
   _____
   _____

—. _____
   _____

SHORT-TERM OBJECTIVES

1. Acknowledge prostitution and describe the reasons for it. (1, 2)

2. Participate in a medical examination to assess general health and sexually transmitted disease status. (3, 4, 5)

3. Obtain ongoing recommended medical care. (6)

4. Describe drug and alcohol usage pattern and history. (7)

5. Accept a referral for drug and alcohol evaluation. (8)

6. Obtain ongoing recommended substance abuse treatment. (8, 9)

7. List the risks associated with continued prostitution. (10, 11)

8. Verbalize feelings of stress, fear, or shame associated with illegal behaviors. (11, 12)

9. Accept referral for counseling to address stress, depression, and self-esteem issues. (2, 12, 13, 14)

THERAPEUTIC INTERVENTIONS

1. Gather a thorough history of client's prostitution.

2. Assist the client in identifying the original and current reasons for his/her behaviors.

3. Refer the client to a physician to rule out any medical conditions that are in need of immediate treatment.

4. Obtain a written confidentiality release from the client to allow for contact with evaluating professionals in order to share information and to obtain the results and recommendations of the evaluations.

5. Provide education regarding sexually transmitted diseases, especially the risks of human immunodeficiency virus (HIV) and hepatitis.

6. Facilitate and monitor the client's access to additional medical services recommended by the examining physician.

10. Report reduced feelings of stress, fear, and shame and increased self-esteem. (13, 14)

11. Describe financial, nutritional, medical, and housing needs. (15)

12. Obtain access to community-based financial, nutritional, medical, and housing resources. (4, 16)

13. Participate in a vocational and educational assessment. (17)

14. Accept referral for vocational or educational training. (18)

15. Agree to sign up for services at employment agencies. (19)

16. Obtain appropriate interviewing and work clothing. (20)

17. Obtain legal employment. (21, 22, 23)

18. Agree to regularly scheduled telephone and/or visitation contact by a caseworker. (24, 25)

—. _____
   _____
—. _____
   _____
—. _____
   _____

7. Explore the client's past and current use of mood-altering substances.

8. Refer the client to a drug and alcohol counselor for an in-depth evaluation for chemical dependence.

9. Facilitate and monitor the client's access to additional inpatient or outpatient substance abuse treatment as recommended by the drug and alcohol evaluation.

10. Emphasize to the client the negative legal and social consequences and medical and safety risks of continuing to engage in prostitution.

11. Assess the client's attitude regarding illegal or antisocial activity and his/her desire to discontinue prostitution.

12. Refer the client for a psychological evaluation to assess his/her mental status.

13. Coordinate the client's obtaining ongoing treatment for psychological problems; refer the client to an appropriate counseling provider.

14. Monitor and reinforce the client's follow-through on obtaining necessary counseling services.

15. Conduct a financial, nutritional, medical, and housing assessment.

16. Link the client to available community supports and resources (e.g., public assis-

tance, food stamps, Medicaid, shelters, or food programs).

17. Refer the client for vocational assessment.

18. Facilitate and monitor the client's access to vocational or educational programming as recommended by the vocational assessment.

19. Refer the client to local employment agencies to sign up for programs.

20. Teach the client about appropriate employment and interviewing attire and refer him/her to agencies that will supply it (e.g., social services, Salvation Army, and thrift stores).

21. Instruct the client or refer him/her for training in correct job application procedures; provide sample practice applications.

22. Instruct the client or refer him/her for training in correct job interviewing techniques; provide opportunities for the client to role-play interviewing.

23. Provide emotional support to the client during employment training and job search.

24. Monitor the client's follow-through to ensure that linkages to community resources are made.

25. Refer the client for ongoing case-management services.

___. _____
      _____
___. _____
      _____
___. _____
      _____

DIAGNOSTIC SUGGESTIONS

Axis I: 296.2x   Major Depressive Disorder, Single Episode
    296.3x   Major Depressive Disorder, Recurrent
    300.4   Dysthymic Disorder
    300.00   Anxiety Disorder NOS
    V62.2   Vocational Problem

_____ _____

_____ _____

Axis II: 301.7   Antisocial Personality Disorder
    V71.09   No Diagnosis on Axis II
    799.9   Diagnosis Deferred on Axis II

_____ _____

_____ _____

PSYCHOSIS

BEHAVIORAL DEFINITIONS

1. Auditory, visual, and/or tactile hallucinations.
2. Delusional thought system.
3. Disorganized speech (e.g., loosening of associations, incoherence, illogical thinking, neologisma, clanging, or repetitive speech).
4. Seriously disturbed affect (e.g., none, blunted, flattened, or inappropriate).
5. Withdrawal from involvement in external world.
6. Grossly disorganized or catatonic behavior.
7. Inability to care for own physical needs adequately.

__. _____
    _____
__. _____
    _____
__. _____
    _____

LONG-TERM GOALS

1. Reduce or eliminate psychotic symptoms.
2. Return to pre-psychotic-episode level of functioning.
3. Access ongoing psychiatric care.
4. Involve self with family.
5. Obtain adequate community support.

—. _____

_____

—. _____

_____

—. _____

_____

SHORT-TERM OBJECTIVES

1. Demonstrate current cognitive, social, and emotional functioning in a mental status exam. (1, 23)

2. Family members provide psychosocial history data. (2)

3. Cooperate with a referral to a physician. (3)

4. Verbalize an understanding that the distressing symptoms are due to a mental illness. (4)

5. Verbalize an understanding of the necessity of taking antipsychotic medication and agree to cooperate with prescribed care. (5, 6, 7)

6. Take antipsychotic medications as prescribed by physician; reporting as to effectiveness and side effects. (5, 8, 9)

7. Monitor self and report a decrease in psychotic symptoms. (7, 10, 11, 12, 13)

8. Show limited social functioning by responding appropriately to friendly encounters. (10, 11, 12, 13)

THERAPEUTIC INTERVENTIONS

1. Complete mental status exam to determine whether inpatient treatment is immediately necessary.

2. Gather a medical and psychiatric history from the client and his/her family members.

3. Refer the client for a medical consultation to evaluate as to organic causes or substance use that may account for his/her psychotic symptoms.

4. Explain to the client the nature of the psychotic process, its biochemical component, and the confusing effect on rational thought.

5. Refer the client for psychiatric evaluation and antipsychotic medication.

6. Educate the client regarding the effectiveness and side effects of the medication and the importance of consistent adherence to the prescribed dosage.

7. Explain to the client the importance of self-monitoring

9. Family members increase their positive support of the client in order to reduce the chances of acute exacerbation of a psychotic episode. (14, 15, 16)

10. Respond favorably to family support. (14, 17)

11. Utilize community-based support programs for financial security, social involvement, and treatment. (18, 19, 20)

12. Client and family members agree on a response plan if the client should start to decompensate. (19, 21, 22, 23)

—. ——————————
    ——————————
—. ——————————
    ——————————
—. ——————————
    ——————————

the medication's effectiveness and reporting back to the professional.

8. Reinforce the client's consistently taking medications.

9. Assess the client's medication for effectiveness and side effects; communicate observations with the prescribing physician.

10. Assess the client for decrease in thought disturbance, for improved social involvement, and for appropriateness of affect; reinforce progress.

11. Reinforce the client's calm, normal appearance, behavior, and speech.

12. Assist the client in reducing threats in the environment (e.g., finding a safer place to live, arranging for regular visits from caseworker, and arranging for family members to call more frequently).

13. Assist the client in restructuring irrational beliefs by reviewing reality-based evidence and misinterpretation.

14. Assess the family support system and encourage the family members' involvement in the client's care to the extent that the client desires it.

15. Provide education to involved family members on the serious nature of the

client's mental illness and
the use of medication.

16. Provide referrals for involved family members to a
support group for families
of psychotic patients.

17. Encourage and reinforce the
client's interaction with
family members.

18. Assess the client's current
community support system
needs.

19. Link the client with psychiatric care and community
programming (e.g., day
treatment, supervized living, case management, or
Compeer).

20. Link the client to financial
assistance programs as
indicated (e.g., Supplemental Security Income, Social
Security Disability, or Medicaid).

21. Educate the client and family members regarding signs
and symptoms of decompen-
sation.

22. Provide the client and family members with a crisis
hotline number and instructions on how and when to
use it if urgent care is necessary for the client's psychological decompensation.

23. Make arrangements for involuntary commitment to
an inpatient psychiatric facility if the client is unable
to care for his/her basic
needs or is harmful to self
or others.

—.   _____

          _____

—.   _____

          _____

—.   _____

          _____

DIAGNOSTIC SUGGESTIONS

Axis I:	297.1	Delusional Disorder
	298.8	Brief Psychotic Disorder
	295.xx	Schizophrenia
	295.70	Schizoaffective Disorder
	296.xx	Bipolar I Disorder
	296.89	Bipolar II Disorder
	296.xx	Major Depressive Disorder
	_____	_____
	_____	_____
Axis II:	V71.09	No Diagnosis on Axis II
	799.9	Diagnosis Deferred on Axis II
	_____	_____
	_____	_____

RAPE VICTIM

BEHAVIORAL DEFINITIONS

1. Self-report of sexual assault victimization.
2. Reports by family, friends, neighbors, or police that the client was a victim of rape.
3. Evidence of rape: bruises; lacerations; broken bones; red, swollen, or torn genitalia; and/or open sores.
4. Intrusive, distressing thoughts, flashbacks, or images that recall the rape.
5. Inability to recall some important aspects of rape.
6. Physiological reactivity and intense distress when exposed to cues that symbolize rape.
7. Fearful isolation and withdrawal in an attempt to protect self from anticipated future victimization.
8. Depressed affect, low energy, sleep disturbance, and tearful spells.
9. Alcohol and/or drug abuse.
10. Inability to enjoy sexual intimacy with desired partner or extreme difficulty in doing so.
11. Positive test for pregnancy, sexually transmitted diseases, and/or HIV.

__. _____
_____

__. _____
_____

__. _____
_____

LONG-TERM GOALS

1. Reduce the negative impact that the rape has had on many aspects of life and return to pretrauma level of functioning.
2. Develop and implement effective coping skills in order to carry out normal responsibilities and participate constructively in relationships.
3. Recall the rape without becoming overwhelmed with negative emotions.
4. Terminate self-destructive behaviors and implement behaviors that promote healing, acceptance of assault, and responsible living.
5. Begin the process of healing from the rape, with resultant enjoyment of appropriate sexual contact.

—. _____

_____

—. _____

_____

—. _____

_____

SHORT-TERM OBJECTIVES

1. Cooperate with a referral to a physician for a medical status assessment. (1, 2)
2. Describe the rape in as much detail as possible. (3, 4)
3. Identify the feelings experienced at the time of the rape. (5)
4. Describe any fears regarding the perpetrator seeking revenge for being reported. (6, 7)
5. Verbalize an understanding of the legal process of police investigation and court proceedings. (8)

THERAPEUTIC INTERVENTIONS

1. Refer the client to a physician to rule out any medical conditions that are in need of immediate treatment.
2. Refer the client to a rape crisis team for completion of a medically administered rape kit for evidentiary purposes.
3. Build rapport with the client through consistent eye contact, unconditional positive regard, warm acceptance, soft voice, conversation about nonthreatening topics, and expressions of reassurance regarding the client's safety.

6. Cooperate with legal authorities under the guidance of an attorney. (9, 10, 11)

7. Verbalize agreement that the responsibility for the rape falls on the perpetrator, not on self. (12, 13)

8. Accept referral to a support group for rape survivors. (14)

9. Accept referral to individual counseling. (15)

10. Describe the amount, history, and frequency of substance abuse used to cope with the trauma. (16)

11. Identify the negative consequences of the substance abuse. (17)

12. Accept referral for drug and/or alcohol evaluation and treatment. (18)

13. Identify sources of support among family and friends. (19)

14. Increase the level of trust of others as shown by more socialization and greater tolerance of intimacy. (20, 21)

15. Report increased ability to accept and initiate appropriate physical contact with others. (22, 23)

__. _____
   _____
__. _____
   _____
__. _____
   _____

4. Slowly and gently explore the details of the rape without pressing the client beyond his/her ability to trust or to cope with emotions associated with the assault.

5. Encourage and support the client in verbally expressing and clarifying his/her feelings at the time of the rape.

6. Assess the client's safety from retaliation by the perpetrator of the rape; facilitate the client's obtaining a place of safety.

7. Facilitate and encourage the client's making contact with legal authorities to obtain protection from further threat of assault and to report the crime.

8. Explain to the client the legal process that will ensue due to the rape.

9. Encourage and empower the client to assert the right to protection from the law by testifying against the perpetrator of the rape.

10. Support the client during the humiliating and stressful legal process.

11. Refer the client to a victim advocacy service provider within the legal system.

12. Confront the client for excusing the perpetrator and reinforce all statements that place clear responsibility on the perpetrator of the rape.

13. Provide a more reality-based view of the circumstances of the rape when the client tends to take on blame for the rape or excuse the perpetrator's actions.

14. Refer the client to a support group for rape survivors.

15. Refer the client to individual counseling to assist in coping with the feelings related to the trauma.

16. Gather data from the client regarding the amount, history, and frequency of substance abuse as a means of coping with the feelings of anger and anxiety associated with the rape experience.

17. Teach the client the negative consequences of abusing substances as a means of coping with guilt, anger, and anxiety (e.g., exacerbation of negative emotions; precipitation of chemical dependence; and precipitation of relational, vocational, and legal problems).

18. Refer the client to a drug and/or alcohol counselor for an evaluation for abuse and dependence.

19. Ask the client to identify people that he/she can turn to for understanding and support.

20. Teach the client the share-check method of building trust in relationships (i.e., share only a little of self

and then check to be sure that the shared data is treated respectfully, kindly, and confidentially; as proof of trustworthiness is verified, share more freely).

21. Encourage and reinforce appropriate social interaction as opposed to withdrawal and isolation.

22. Encourage the client to give and receive appropriate touches, helping to define what is appropriate.

23. Ask the client to practice initiating touching (e.g., holding hands, giving partner a back rub, or hugging a friend) one or two times per week.

—. _____
    _____
    _____

—. _____
    _____

—. _____
    _____

DIAGNOSTIC SUGGESTIONS

Axis I:	309.81	Posttraumatic Stress Disorder
	309.xx	Adjustment Disorder
	308.3	Acute Stress Disorder
	296.xx	Major Depressive Disorder
	_____	_____
	_____	_____
Axis II:	V71.09	No Diagnosis on Axis II
	799.9	Diagnosis Deferred on Axis II
	_____	_____
	_____	_____

SEXUAL ABUSE PERPETRATOR

BEHAVIORAL DEFINITIONS

1. Loss of control of sexual and aggressive impulses, resulting in rape, sodomy, fondling, frotteurism, exhibitionism, and/or fetishes.
2. Recurrent, intense, sexually arousing fantasies and sexual urges that cause distress or impairment in social, family, and/or occupational functioning.
3. History of being a victim of sexual abuse in childhood.
4. Pervasive pattern of inappropriate sexualization of relationships.
5. Failure to establish a lasting, meaningful, intimate relationship with an adult of the opposite sex.
6. Pattern of creating dependency in a minor-age victim and then using the trust for own sexual gratification.
7. Pattern of forcing sexual contact on victim with acts or threats of violence to obtain compliance.
8. Use of verbally abusive language, intended to berate, threaten, intimidate, or hurt others.
9. Pattern of treating children as "little adults."
10. Failure to function as a consistently concerned and responsible parent.
11. Abuse of alcohol and/or drugs.
12. Display of little or no remorse for abusive behavior.
13. Consistent pattern of blaming others for what happens to self.

—. _____

_____

—. _____

_____

—. _____

_____

LONG-TERM GOALS

1. Eliminate sexually and physically aggressive acts.
2. Accept responsibility for own actions.
3. Demonstrate appropriate parenting skills.
4. Reduce substance abuse.
5. Eliminate all contact with victim target group (e.g., male children or female adolescents).
6. Inform victims of medical status regarding sexually transmitted diseases.

__. _____

   _____

__. _____

   _____

__. _____

   _____

SHORT-TERM OBJECTIVES

1. Describe the physically and sexually aggressive acts that have been exhibited over the past 12 months. (1, 2)
2. Verbalize an understanding of the necessity of eliminating sexually abusive behaviors. (3, 4, 5)
3. Accept referral to a sexual perpetrators group. (6, 7)
4. Accept referral for individual therapy to eliminate sexually aggressive behaviors. (6, 8)
5. Accept referral to attend parenting classes. (9)
6. Describe the amount, frequency, and history of alcohol or drug use. (10)

THERAPEUTIC INTERVENTIONS

1. Gather a history of the client's instances of sexually and physically aggressive behavior.
2. Report to children's protective services if a child was sexually abused; report to the local police department if an adult was abused.
3. Confront the client's lack of sensitivity to the needs and feelings of others.
4. Affirm the reality of the abusive, illegal nature of the sexual contact the client was having with the victim.
5. Inform the client of the legal mandate for counselors to report child sexual abuse to the proper authori-

7. Accept referral for substance abuse evaluation and counseling. (6, 11)

8. Accept referral to a legal advocate. (12)

9. Eliminate contact with the target group for abuse (e.g., male children or female adolescents). (13, 14)

10. Accept referral to a medical clinic for assessment for sexually transmitted diseases and acquired immunodeficiency syndrome (AIDS). (15)

11. Attend supervised visitation with the child. (14, 16)

12. Report as to follow-through on recommendations for treatment. (17, 18, 19)

—. _____
   _____

—. _____
   _____

—. _____
   _____

ties for the protection of the child.

6. Obtain appropriate consent forms to make referrals for the client for treatment of his/her sexual abuse behavior.

7. Locate treatment options and refer the client for group therapy treatment for sexual perpetrators.

8. Refer the client for individual mental health counseling.

9. Refer the client to community-based parenting classes to increase his/her skills and understanding in dealing with children.

10. Explore whether the client's substance abuse pattern may be problematic and in need of future assessment.

11. Refer the client to a substance abuse counselor for evaluation and treatment of chemical dependence.

12. Refer the client to a court appointed or private lawyer to assist him/her in reacting to the legal charges that will result from the criminal sexual conduct.

13. Inform the client that he/she must avoid contact with the victim and others in that target group.

14. Inform legal authorities of the need for stipulations from the court in order to deny the client unsupervised contact with the vic-

tim and others in the target group.

15. Refer the client to a community-based medical clinic for evaluation for sexually transmitted diseases and/or AIDS.

16. If the court orders it, arrange for the client's supervised visitation with the child victim.

17. Monitor the client's follow-through on all referrals and evaluations.

18. Solicit progress reports from all service providers as to the client's attendance, cooperation, and progress with treatment.

19. Write a report to the court addressing the client's progress and improvement.

__. _____
_____

__. _____
_____

__. _____
_____

DIAGNOSTIC SUGGESTIONS

Axis I:	302.4	Exhibitionism
	302.81	Fetishism
	302.89	Frotteurism
	302.2	Pedophilia
	302.84	Sexual Sadism
	302.82	Voyeurism
	_____	_____
	_____	_____

Axis II: 301.7   Antisocial Personality Disorder
301.81   Narcissistic Personality Disorder
V71.09   No Diagnosis on Axis II
799.9   Diagnosis Deferred on Axis II

_____   _____

_____   _____

SEXUAL ABUSE VICTIM (CHILD)

BEHAVIORAL DEFINITIONS

1. Self-report of being sexually abused.
2. Reports by family, neighbors, friends, teachers, or police that the child has been a victim of sexual abuse.
3. Evidence of sexual abuse: bruises; bone fractures; red, swollen, or torn genitalia; and/or open sores.
4. Depressed affect, low energy, sleep disturbance, and tearful spells.
5. Agitation and irritability.
6. Fearful isolation and withdrawal in an attempt to protect self from anticipated future abuse.
7. Appearance of regressive behaviors (e.g., thumb sucking, baby talk, and bed-wetting).
8. Sexualized or seductive behavior with younger children, peers, or adults (e.g., provocative exhibition of genitalia, fondling, mutual masturbation, or anal or vaginal penetration).

—. _____

_____

—. _____

_____

—. _____

_____

LONG-TERM GOALS

1. Obtain immediate protection from all further sexual victimization.
2. Live in a safe environment without fear of reprisal.
3. Overcome mood disruption and return to a sense of joy, peace, and security.

4. Family members provide emotional support to the sexually abused child.
5. Eliminate all inappropriate sexual behaviors.

—. _____

_____

_____

—. _____

_____

_____

—. _____

_____

SHORT-TERM OBJECTIVES

1. Describe the details regarding the nature, extent, frequency, and perpetrator of abuse. (1, 2, 3)
2. Parents provide emotional support to the victimized child. (4, 5)
3. Participate in a medical examination to assess the consequences of sexual abuse. (5, 6, 7)
4. Obtain ongoing recommended medical care. (7)
5. Describe any fears regarding the perpetrator seeking revenge for being reported. (8, 9, 10)
6. Verbalize an understanding of the need to contact legal authorities for self-protection. (11)
7. Move to a nonabusive living environment. (9, 10, 12)
8. Perpetrator of abuse moves out of the home to guarantee the safety of the child. (13, 14)

THERAPEUTIC INTERVENTIONS

1. Build rapport with the client through consistent eye contact, unconditional positive regard, warm acceptance, soft voice, conversation about nonthreatening topics, and expressions of reassurance regarding the client's safety.
2. Slowly explore the details of the client's abuse without pressing the client beyond his/her level of trust or capacity to cope.
3. Change the subject to less threatening topics before gently returning for more open probing of the facts of the abuse.
4. Involve parents in the assessment process and encourage their emotional support for the child.
5. Obtain a written confidentiality release from the parents to allow for contact with the evaluating professional in order to share in-

9. Agree to testify against the perpetrator of the abuse in court as appropriate. (15)

10. Verbalize agreement that responsibility for the abuse falls on the perpetrator, not on self. (16, 17)

11. Cooperate with a psychological evaluation to assess the consequences of the sexual abuse. (5, 18)

12. Accept a referral to counseling to heal the emotional scars resulting from the abuse. (18, 19, 20)

13. Verbalize feelings about structured, closely supervised visits with the family member who perpetrated the abuse. (21, 22)

14. Verbalize feelings toward the perpetrator of the abuse. (23)

15. Parents attend classes that teach effective parenting techniques and establishment of proper boundaries. (24, 25, 30)

16. Perpetrator follows through with treatment referral. (26, 27, 28, 30)

17. Attend a survivors' support group. (29, 30)

18. Agree to regularly scheduled telephone and/or visitation contact by a caseworker. (30, 31)

formation regarding the abuse and to obtain the results and recommendations of the evaluation.

6. Refer the client to a physician for examination of the consequences of the abuse.

7. Facilitate and monitor the client's access to more medical services as recommended by the examining physician.

8. Assess the client's safety from retaliation by the perpetrator of the abuse.

9. If the current caregivers are unable to provide a safe environment, explore temporarily removing the client to the custody of other family members who are able to provide a safe environment.

10. If the current caregivers are unable to provide a safe environment and no other family members are available for the client, refer him/her to the foster care system.

11. Explain to the client why it is necessary to contact legal authorities to obtain protection from further abuse; facilitate opening a case with the children's protective services agency.

12. Monitor and support the client's move to a safe environment; meet with the client to encourage and reassure him/her and answer his/her questions.

__. _____

_____

__. _____

_____

__. _____

_____

13. Facilitate a court order for removal of the perpetrator of sexual abuse from the client's home; monitor its enforcement.

14. Monitor the client's ongoing safety for any incidents or threats of further abuse.

15. Provide emotional and moral support for the client as he/she follows through with legal testimony against the perpetrator of the abuse if required.

16. Confront the client for excusing the perpetrator and reinforce all statements that place clear responsibility for the abuse on the perpetrator.

17. Provide a more reality-based view of the circumstances of the abuse when the client tends to take on blame for the abuse or excuse the perpetrator's actions.

18. Refer the client for a psychological evaluation to assess emotional and/or cognitive consequences of the abuse.

19. Coordinate the client's obtaining ongoing treatment for psychological problems resulting from the abuse; refer the client to an appropriate counseling provider.

20. Monitor the parents' follow-through on obtaining necessary counseling services for the client.

21. Explore the future of the relationship with the perpe-

trator of the abuse, especially if the perpetrator is a family member or "friend."

22. Facilitate closely supervised visits between the client and the family member who was the perpetrator of the sexual abuse.

23. Explore the client's emotional reaction to the abuse, allowing for a free expression of feelings in an accepting atmosphere of support.

24. Insist on and teach the need for proper boundaries between an adult and a child or an older child and a younger child.

25. Refer the parents to an effective-parenting class.

26. Require the perpetrator to attend and actively participate in a sexual offenders' group.

27. Refer the perpetrator for individual counseling.

28. Obtain a court order to require the perpetrator to pursue the psychological treatment recommended.

29. Refer the client to a survivors' support group with other children to assist him/her in realizing that he/she is not alone in having experienced sexual abuse.

30. Monitor the client and family members to ensure that linkages to recommend treatment resources are made.

31. Explain the necessity of accepting case-management services as available.

—. _____

_____

—. _____

_____

—. _____

_____

DIAGNOSTIC SUGGESTIONS

Axis I:

309.0	Adjustment Disorder With Depressed Mood
309.24	Adjustment Disorder With Anxiety
296.2x	Major Depressive Disorder, Single Episode
300.02	Generalized Anxiety Disorder
V61.21	Sexual Abuse of Child
308.3	Acute Stress Disorder
309.81	Posttraumatic Stress Disorder
_____	_____
_____	_____

Axis II:

V71.09	No Diagnosis on Axis II
799.9	Diagnosis Deferred on Axis II
_____	_____
_____	_____

SUICIDE ATTEMPT

BEHAVIORAL DEFINITIONS

1. Intentional attempt to end life (e.g., overdose, self-inflicted wound, refusing to eat, or jumping in front of a moving vehicle).
2. Feelings of depression and despair.
3. Lack of hope or future orientation.
4. Social withdrawal and/or conflict.
5. Feelings of worthlessness.
6. Suffering from a recent loss (e.g., financial security, significant relationship, freedom, employment, or shelter).
7. Lack of an adequate support system.

__. _____
   _____
__. _____
   _____
__. _____
   _____

LONG-TERM GOALS

1. Stabilize the suicidal crisis.
2. Obtain the appropriate level of care to safely address the suicidal crisis.
3. Overcome depression and suicidal ideation and return to a sense of joy, peace, and security.
4. Reestablish a sense of hope for self and life.
5. Develop adaptive methods to cope with the pressures of life.
6. Develop future-oriented goals.
7. Increase familial and social support systems.

8. Increase community support.
9. Develop a suicide prevention plan in case suicidal ideation should return.

___. _____

_____

_____

___. _____

_____

_____

___. _____

_____

SHORT-TERM OBJECTIVES

THERAPEUTIC INTERVENTIONS

1. Participate in a medical examination to assess the physical consequences of the suicide attempt. (1)

2. Cooperate with an assessment of current mental status and need for antidepressants. (3, 4, 5)

3. Accept the level of care necessary to safely address mental status and immediate medical needs. (2, 3, 4, 5)

4. Accept psychiatric follow-up and counseling to heal the emotional scars that led to the suicide attempt. (6, 7)

5. Identify the circumstances that led to the onset of suicidal feelings. (8)

6. Verbalize feelings surrounding the suicide attempt. (8, 9)

7. Demonstrate improved problem-solving and relaxation skills. (10, 11)

8. Identify and verbalize reasons to live. (12, 13)

1. Refer the client to a physician for medical examination and stabilization of physical consequences due to the suicide attempt.

2. Build rapport with the client through consistent eye contact, unconditional positive regard, warm acceptance, and soft voice.

3. Conduct a current mental status exam of the client to determine the level of psychiatric care immediately needed.

4. Refer the client to a physician for assessment of his/her need for antidepressants and/or inpatient treatment.

5. Educate the client about depression.

6. Educate the client about antidepressant effectiveness and side effects and how to self-monitor them.

9. Identify future goals. (13)
10. Participate in family counseling as appropriate to improve family functioning and support. (14)
11. Educate the family members about the need to increase their sensitivity to the client's depression and to monitor for indicators of suicidal ideation. (14, 15, 16)
12. Increase involvement in social and therapeutic activities. (17, 18, 19, 20)
13. Accept referral to a community support group. (19, 20, 21, 22)
14. Apply for financial aid to obtain ongoing psychiatric and medical services. (23, 24)
15. Establish a prevention plan in case suicidal ideation should return. (25, 26, 27)

—. _____
_____
—. _____
_____
—. _____
_____

7. Monitor the client's follow-through with mental health treatment and medication compliance, effectiveness, and side effects.
8. Assist the client in identifying reasons for the suicide attempt.
9. Slowly explore the client's feelings that led to the suicide attempt.
10. Teach the client problem-solving skills (e.g., brainstorming and evaluating alternative solutions, discussing issues with others, and developing an action plan with small steps toward the goal) to assist him/her in identifying alternatives to suicide.
11. Teach the client techniques of deep breathing, muscle relaxation, and positive imagery as stress-reduction mechanisms.
12. Assist the client in identifying reasons to live.
13. Assist the client in identifying goals to reinforce a future orientation.
14. Provide family therapy or refer the client and family members for family therapy in order to identify familial factors contributing to the suicide attempt.
15. Educate the family members about signs of depression, antidepressant side effects, and methods of offering emotional support to the client.

16. Refer the family to the National Association for the Mentally Impaired for access to family support available in the community.

17. Educate the client as to the services available in the community (e.g., day treatment, partial hospitalization, supportive housing, and support groups).

18. Explore with the client opportunities for increased social contacts with family and friends and community activities.

19. Link the client to community support programs and activities as available and desired.

20. Suggest that the client accept case-management services as available.

21. Monitor the client to ensure that linkages are made.

22. Obtain a written release of confidential information from the client to allow for contact with specific professionals and/or programs in order to facilitate referrals and linkages.

23. Refer the client for available financial support resources as eligible and appropriate (e.g., Medicaid, Supplemental Security Income, or Social Security Disability).

24. Ensure that the client has resources to obtain prescriptions, linking to religiously based monetary aid providers (e.g., Salvation

Army or Catholic Charities)
for assistance if necessary.

25. Provide the client with a
local 24-hour crisis number
and instructions on how to
use the service.

26. Assist the client in identifying a plan to access immediate support (e.g., phone
numbers for crisis center,
social worker, family member, and emergency room) in
case suicidal ideation
should return.

27. Develop a contract with the
client for no self-harm and
for contact with support
services if suicidal urges
return.

__. _____
   _____
__. _____
   _____
__. _____
   _____

DIAGNOSTIC SUGGESTIONS

Axis I: 296.xx   Bipolar I Disorder
            296.2x   Major Depressive Disorder, Single Episode
            296.3x   Major Depressive Disorder, Recurrent
            296.89   Bipolar II Disorder
            300.4   Dysthymic Disorder
            _____   _____
            _____   _____

Axis II: 301.83   Borderline Personality Disorder
            V71.09   No Diagnosis on Axis II
            799.9   Diagnosis Deferred on Axis II
            _____   _____
            _____   _____

SUICIDE VICTIM'S FAMILY

BEHAVIORAL DEFINITIONS

1. Suicide of an immediate family member.
2. Feelings of confusion and despair.
3. Anger directed at suicide victim.
4. Feelings of guilt and responsibility related to the suicide.
5. Depression and crying spells.
6. Loss of appetite.
7. Sleep disruption.
8. Impaired concentration.
9. Feelings of isolation and aloneness.

___. _____
_____
___. _____
_____
___. _____
_____

LONG-TERM GOALS

1. Overcome initial shock and begin healthy grieving process.
2. Stabilize the family system.
3. Diminish symptoms of depression and feelings of grief.
4. Establish adequate emotional support system.
5. Return to normal routine.

—. _____
   _____
   _____

—. _____
   _____
   _____

—. _____
   _____
   _____

SHORT-TERM OBJECTIVES

1. State the facts related to the family member's suicide. (1)
2. Identify and express feelings related to the family member's suicide. (2, 3, 4)
3. Provide genogram information. (3, 4)
4. Verbalize an understanding of the grief process. (5)
5. Demonstrate current social and emotional functioning in a mental status exam. (6)
6. Provide psychosocial history data for each family member. (7)
7. Cooperate with referral to a physician if indicated. (8)
8. Take psychotropic mediation consistently as prescribed and report as to its effectiveness and side effects. (9)
9. Implement relaxation techniques to reduce stress levels. (10)
10. Identify and contact sources of emotional support. (4, 11, 12)

THERAPEUTIC INTERVENTIONS

1. Hold a session with all family members present to explore the facts related to the family member's suicide.
2. Explore each family member's feelings, giving each member an opportunity to speak.
3. Assess the current level of family functioning.
4. Develop a genogram for immediate and extended family members and assess current family dynamics and potential for mutual support.
5. Educate family members about the stages of the grief process and about what feelings they might expect within themselves and toward each other during the process.
6. Complete a mental status exam for each family member to determine whether immediate psychological treatment is necessary.
7. Gather a medical and psychiatric history of each family member.

11. Accept referral to a local grief support group. (13, 14, 15)

12. Report improved family functioning. (16)

13. Verbalize positive and happy memories of the deceased family member without feelings of depression. (17, 18)

—. _____
_____

—. _____
_____

—. _____
_____

8. Refer family members for psychiatric evaluation and assessment for psychotropic medication.

9. Monitor psychotropic medication prescription compliance, effectiveness, and side effects.

10. Teach deep muscle relaxation exercises and deep-breathing exercises to reduce reactive stress.

11. Explore the family's social system for those who are potential sources of support and comfort (e.g., friends, family, and church members).

12. Encourage contact with identified sources of emotional support.

13. Educate family members about grief support groups available for families of suicide victims.

14. Refer the family members to a grief support group.

15. Monitor linkage to ensure that family members attend the support group and to remove any barriers to this follow-through.

16. Perform an ongoing assessment of family dynamics and functioning, giving assistance or referrals when required.

17. Provide opportunities for family members to speak of positive memories of the deceased family member.

18. Invite the family members to return for additional supportive counseling services if desired at a future time, or refer the family members for more intense family therapy.

—. _____

_____

—. _____

_____

—. _____

_____

DIAGNOSTIC SUGGESTIONS

Axis I:	V62.82	Bereavement
	_____	_____
	_____	_____
Axis II:	V71.09	No Diagnosis on Axis II
	799.9	Diagnosis Deferred on Axis II
	_____	_____
	_____	_____

TEEN PREGNANCY

BEHAVIORAL DEFINITIONS

1. Pregnancy resulting from a long-term relationship.
2. Pregnancy resulting from short-term relationship.
3. Relationship with the father of the unborn child ongoing and supportive.
4. Relationship with the father of the unborn child nonsupportive and terminated.
5. Uncertainty regarding the identity of the father of the unborn child.
6. Ambivalence regarding whether to abort the pregnancy.
7. Desire to complete the pregnancy but with feelings of confusion and anxiety regarding the future.
8. Feelings of embarrassment and shame regarding the pregnancy.
9. Denial regarding the implications that the pregnancy brings to current and future life.
10. Lack of a support system to provide guidance and assistance during the pregnancy.
11. Lack of follow-through on obtaining adequate prenatal care.
12. Desire to abort the pregnancy but with feelings of confusion regarding how to safely implement the decision.
13. Desire to release the child for adoption but lack of information as to how to proceed.
14. Withdrawal from school due to the pregnancy.
15. Severe conflict in family due to the pregnancy.

___. _____

_____

___. _____

_____

___. _____

_____

LONG-TERM GOALS

1. Make a decision regarding the termination or completion of the pregnancy.
2. Complete abortion if termination of the pregnancy is selected.
3. Obtain prenatal care consistently if completion of the pregnancy is selected.
4. Decide whether to keep the infant or release it for adoption if completion of the pregnancy is selected.
5. Use birth control upon termination or completion of the pregnancy.
6. Continue education program during the pregnancy.
7. Family members terminate blaming and punishing and show support for the pregnant teen.

—. _____

_____

_____

—. _____

_____

_____

—. _____

_____

SHORT-TERM OBJECTIVES

1. Confirm the pregnancy and the duration of pregnancy. (1)
2. Identify feelings about the pregnancy. (2, 3, 4)
3. List the pregnancy response options and the expected consequences of each potential response. (5, 6)
4. Make a decision about completing or terminating the pregnancy. (6, 7, 8, 22)
5. Attend counseling sessions to aid in coping with the stress of this life crisis. (9, 10)

THERAPEUTIC INTERVENTIONS

1. Make a medical referral to confirm the client's pregnancy and its duration.
2. Explore the facts and the client's feelings related to her becoming pregnant.
3. Explore the future of the client's relationship with the father of the unborn child.
4. Explore family dynamics that may have contributed to the client's behavior.
5. Provide the client with a range of options regarding her pregnancy (i.e., abor-

6. Access medical and prenatal care on a consistent basis. (11)

7. Attend educational classes on a consistent basis. (12, 13, 14)

8. Agree to attend parenting education classes. (15)

9. Verbalize realistic expectations for life after delivery. (15, 16, 17)

10. Agree to consistently use birth control postpregnancy. (18)

11. Verbalize a decision for abortion or release of parental rights that is free of guilt. (19, 20, 21, 22)

___. _____
   _____

___. _____
   _____

___. _____
   _____

tion, adoption, or keeping the baby).

6. Teach the client problem-solving techniques (e.g., brainstorming options and analyzing the pros and cons of each; utilizing outside resources to review the options together) that she can apply to this crisis in order to improve her decision making.

7. Hold a session with the parents and boyfriend to include them in the problem-solving process as appropriate.

8. Assist the parents in providing emotional support to the client while she struggles with a very important decision.

9. Discuss the advantages of counseling and refer the client for psychological counseling to assist in managing the stress associated with the crisis.

10. Facilitate and monitor the client's obtaining counseling services to deal with the stress of the crisis.

11. Refer the client for medical and prenatal care.

12. Stress the importance of the client's continuing her education.

13. Reinforce the client's consistent school attendance.

14. Coordinate with school officials to ensure that the client's education continues.

15. Provide parenting education or refer the client for it if she plans to keep the baby.

16. Assist the client in setting realistic postpregnancy goals that take into account all the responsibilities of caring for a totally dependent infant.

17. Review with the client all potential sources of emotional and child care support after the delivery.

18. Discuss the importance of using birth control postpregnancy; refer the client to resources that provide free access to birth control measures.

19. Explore the client's moral or religious values with regard to abortion in order to assess for a possible conflict of conscience in implementing an abortion.

20. Refer the client for abortion counseling and medical services.

21. Explore whether the client's family members will be judgmental regarding her abortion decision; assess the client's coping skills for this added stress.

22. Reinforce the client's right to make her own informed decision as to a response to her pregnancy.

___. _____
      _____

___. _____
      _____

___. _____
      _____

DIAGNOSTIC SUGGESTIONS

Axis I: 309.0   Adjustment Disorder With Depressed Mood
              309.24   Adjustment Disorder With Anxiety
              312.9   Disruptive Behavior Disorder NOS
              V61.9   Relational Problem Related to a Mental
                                    Disorder or General Medical Condition
              V61.20   Parent–Child Relational Problem

              _____   _____

              _____   _____

Axis II: V71.09   No Diagnosis on Axis II

              _____   _____

              _____   _____

TRUANCY

BEHAVIORAL DEFINITIONS

1. Does not attend school at all or leaves school during school hours without permission.
2. Has a home environment that is chaotic and conflictual.
3. Has parents who demonstrate a lack of consistent supervision of children.
4. Has a conflictual relationship with parents.
5. Has a learning disability that results in academic struggles and failure.
6. Experiences anxiety, phobia, and/or panic attacks at school.
7. Has feelings of depression and possibly suicidal ideations.
8. Refuses to follow adult directives.
9. Leaves home overnight or longer without permission.
10. Abuses alcohol and/or drugs.
11. Interacts with a negative peer group.
12. Has parents who enforce household rules inconsistently.

__. _____
   _____

__. _____
   _____
   _____

__. _____
   _____

LONG-TERM GOALS

1. Attend school for the entire day on a regular basis.
2. Stabilize the home environment and increase harmony in the family.

3. Parents increase positive involvement with and supervision of their children.
4. Reduce or eliminate anxiety or depressive symptoms.
5. Obtain testing to identify learning disability.
6. Follow household rules, showing respect for authority and bonding with the family.
7. Terminate use of alcohol and/or drugs.
8. Interact with a positive peer group.

—. _____
_____
—. _____
_____
—. _____
_____

SHORT-TERM OBJECTIVES

1. Provide information regarding history of and causes for truancy. (1, 2)

2. School officials provide facts regarding the client's school attendance. (3)

3. Accept referral to a physician for a medication evaluation and treatment. (4)

4. Implement social, recreational, and therapeutic activities to reduce stress in a prosocial manner. (5, 6)

5. The client and parents agree to enter family therapy together to resolve issues of conflict within the family. (7)

6. Parents implement social and recreational activities, cognitive restructuring, and

THERAPEUTIC INTERVENTIONS

1. Gather data from the client regarding the history of and causes for his/her truancy.

2. Explore the factors influencing the client's decision to be truant (e.g., fear of peers, substance abuse, family conflicts, negative peer group, learning problems, or mental illness).

3. Contact school officials regarding their perspective on the client's truancy.

4. Refer the client for a medical consultation to evaluate the need for medication for anxiety and/or depression.

5. Teach the client behavioral techniques to manage stress (e.g., keeping a journal, listening to or playing music,

deep muscle relaxation techniques to reduce tension. (8, 9)

7. Accept referral to a psychologist for educational and psychological assessment. (10)

8. Parents indicate a need and desire to learn skills to manage the client's behavior. (11, 12, 13)

9. Parents attend classes on parenting skills. (14)

10. Cooperate with a drug and alcohol evaluation. (15)

11. Participate in substance abuse treatment. (16)

12. Identify stress-related problems, generate solutions, and choose the best solution. (17, 18)

13. Demonstrate improved eye contact, initiation of social contact, and respectful communication skills. (19, 20)

14. Attend all classes in school on a daily basis. (21, 22, 23)

15. Discuss any fears related to school attendance. (2, 22, 24)

16. Verbalize an understanding of and respect for family rules. (11, 25)

—. _____

_____

—. _____

_____

—. _____

_____

exercise, deep muscle relaxation, calling a friend, or talking to a school counselor).

6. Assist the client in identifying current problems that generate tension and may contribute to truancy.

7. Perform family therapy to reduce conflict within the family or refer the client and parents for family therapy.

8. Help the parents develop a behavioral coping plan for their personal relaxation (e.g., physical exercise, social engagements, or recreational activities).

9. Teach parents relaxation techniques (e.g., deep breathing and muscle relaxation) as a means of reducing stress and irritability.

10. Refer the client to a psychologist for an evaluation of cognitive strengths and weaknesses, as well as educational achievement levels and learning disability symptoms.

11. Provide parents with information about the benefits of enforcing rules consistently.

12. Urge the parents to read books on effective parenting techniques (e.g., *Family Rules* [Kaye], *Ten Things Every Parent Needs to Know* [Paleg], or *Parents and Adolescents* [Forgatch and Patterson]).

13. Provide information to the parents regarding the effective use of consequences and rewards to manage children's behavior (see *1-2-3 Magic: Training Your Preschoolers and Preteens to Do What You Want* [Phelan]).

14. Refer the parents to community-based parenting classes to increase their parenting skills and their understanding in dealing with their children.

15. Evaluate the client for chemical abuse and dependence or refer the client to a drug and alcohol counselor for an evaluation.

16. Treat the client for substance abuse or refer the client for treatment.

17. Assist the client in learning the steps of effective problem-solving (e.g., identify the problem, brainstorm possible solutions, evaluate the pros and cons of each solution, and select the best solution).

18. Use role-playing, modeling, and behavioral rehearsal to allow the client to practice problem solving and/or communication skills; give feedback, redirection, reinforcement as indicated.

19. Assist the client in learning social skills (e.g., eye contact, appropriate greetings, pleasant and respectful conversation, and showing interest in others).

20. Assign the client to initiate one peer social contact per day and to keep a journal of the results; process the experience.

21. Emphasize to the client the negative consequences of continued truancy.

22. Explore for any situational stressor that may be precipitating truancy; process and resolve.

23. Monitor and reinforce the client's consistent attendance at all classes.

24. Address the client's causes for fear of the school environment (e.g., academic failure, peer conflict, or social rejection); refer for further treatment if necessary.

25. Hold a family session where the rules of the family can be clarified and reinforced; solicit the client's cooperation with those rules.

—. _____
_____

—. _____
_____

—. _____
_____

DIAGNOSTIC SUGGESTIONS

Axis I: 313.81   Oppositional Defiant Disorder
309.21   Separation Anxiety Disorder
300.23   Social Phobia
300.01   Panic Disorder Without Agoraphobia

300.21	Panic Disorder With Agoraphobia
300.22	Agoraphobia Without History of Panic Disorder
296.xx	Major Depressive Disorder
V61.20	Parent–Child Relational Problem
_____	_____
_____	_____

Axis II:

V71.09	No Diagnosis on Axis II
799.9	Diagnosis Deferred on Axis II
_____	_____
_____	_____

Appendix

INDEX OF DSM-IV™ CODES ASSOCIATED WITH PRESENTING PROBLEMS

Acute Stress Disorder   **308.3**
Assault Victim
Older Adult Abuse
Rape Victim
Sexual Abuse Victim (Child)

Adjustment Disorder   **309.xx**
Assault Victim
Rape Victim

**Adjustment Disorder With
Anxiety**   **309.24**
Child Physical/Verbal Abuse
Employment Conflicts
Family Conflict
Foster Care Maladjustment (Child)
Housing Inadequacies
Legal Involvement
Murder Victim's Family
Nutritional Risk/Food Insecurity
Older Adult Abuse
Older Adult Residential Adjustment
Physical/Cognitive Disability
Poverty
Sexual Abuse Victim (Child)
Teen Pregnancy

**Adjustment Disorder With
Depressed Mood**   **309.0**
Child Physical/Verbal Abuse
Employment Conflicts

Family Conflict
Foster Care Maladjustment (Child)
Housing Inadequacies
Juvenile Runaway
Legal Involvement
Murder Victim's Family
Nutritional Risk/Food Insecurity
Older Adult Abuse
Older Adult Isolation
Older Adult Residential Adjustment
Physical/Cognitive Disability
Poverty
Sexual Abuse Victim (Child)
Teen Pregnancy

**Adjustment Disorder With
Disturbance of Conduct**   **309.3**
Assaultive Behavior
Foster Care Maladjustment (Child)
Juvenile Runaway
Legal Involvement
Murder Victim's Family

**Adjustment Disorder With
Mixed Anxiety and
Depressed Mood**   **309.28**
Employment Conflicts
Family Conflict
Foster Care Maladjustment (Child)
Housing Inadequacies
Nutritional Risk/Food Insecurity

Older Adult Residential Adjustment
Physical/Cognitive Disability
Poverty

**Adjustment Disorder With
Mixed Disturbance
of Emotions and Conduct   309.4**
Foster Care Maladjustment (Child)
Juvenile Runaway

**Adjustment Disorder
Unspecified   309.9**
Foster Care Maladjustment (Child)

Adult Antisocial Behavior   V71.01
Assaultive Behavior
Drug Abuse/Dependence
Legal Involvement
Partner Abuse

**Age-Related Cognitive
Decline   780.9**
Physical/Cognitive Disability

**Agoraphobia Without
History of Panic Disorder   300.22**
Truancy

Alcohol Abuse   305.00
Alcohol Abuse/Dependence
Juvenile Delinquency

Alcohol Dependence   303.90
Alcohol Abuse/Dependence
Assaultive Behavior
Juvenile Delinquency

Amnestic Disorder NOS   294.8
Physical/Cognitive Disability

**Antisocial Personality
Disorder   301.7**
Alcohol Abuse/Dependence
Assaultive Behavior
Child Physical/Verbal Abuse
Drug Abuse/Dependence
Family Conflict
Legal Involvement
Partner Abuse
Prostitution
Sexual Abuse Perpetrator

Anxiety Disorder NOS   300.00
Assault Victim
Employment Conflicts
Family Conflict
Housing Inadequacies
Nutritional Risk/Food Insecurity
Physical/Cognitive Disability
Poverty
Prostitution

**Attention-Deficit/Hyperactivity
Disorder, Predominantly
Hyperactive-Impulsive
Type   314.01**
Juvenile Delinquency

**Avoidant Personality
Disorder   301.82**
Child Physical/Verbal Abuse
Older Adult Abuse
Older Adult Isolation

Bereavement   V62.82
Murder Victim's Family
Suicide Victim's Family

Bipolar I Disorder   296.xx
Employment Conflicts
Homelessness
Housing Inadequacies
Nutritional Risk/Food Insecurity
Partner Abuse
Poverty
Psychosis
Suicide Attempt

Bipolar II Disorder   296.89
Family Conflict
Homelessness
Partner Abuse
Psychosis
Suicide Attempt

Bipolar Disorder NOS   296.80
Employment Conflicts
Housing Inadequacies
Nutritional Risk/Food Insecurity
Poverty

**Borderline Intellectual
Functioning   V62.89**
Neglect of Child

**Borderline Personality
Disorder**   301.83
  Assaultive Behavior
  Family Conflict
  Suicide Attempt

Brief Psychotic Disorder   298.8
  Psychosis

Cannabis Abuse   305.20
  Drug Abuse/Dependence
  Juvenile Delinquency

Cannabis Dependence   304.30
  Drug Abuse/Dependence
  Juvenile Delinquency

Cocaine Abuse   305.60
  Drug Abuse/Dependence

Cocaine Dependence   304.20
  Drug Abuse/Dependence

Cognitive Disorder NOS   294.9
  Physical/Cognitive Disability

Conduct Disorder   312.8
  Assaultive Behavior
  Juvenile Delinquency
  Negative Peer Group (Adolescent)

Delusional Disorder   297.1
  Homelessness
  Psychosis

**Dementia Due to General
Medical Condition**   294.1
  Physical/Cognitive Disability

**Dependent Personality
Disorder**   301.6
  Older Adult Abuse

Depressive Disorder NOS   311
  Family Conflict
  Neglect of Child

**Diagnosis Deferred
on Axis II**   799.9
  Alcohol Abuse/Dependence
  Assaultive Behavior
  Assault Victim

  Employment Conflicts
  Family Conflict
  Foster Care Maladjustment (Child)
  Homelessness
  Housing Inadequacies
  Murder Victim's Family
  Neglect of Child
  Nutritional Risk/Food Insecurity
  Partner Abuse
  Physical/Cognitive Disability
  Poverty
  Prostitution
  Psychosis
  Rape Victim
  Sexual Abuse Perpetrator
  Sexual Abuse Victim (Child)
  Suicide Attempt
  Suicide Victim's Family
  Truancy

**Disruptive Behavior
Disorder NOS**   312.9
  Juvenile Delinquency
  Negative Peer Group (Adolescent)
  Teen Pregnancy

Dysthymic Disorder   300.4
  Family Conflict
  Prostitution
  Suicide Attempt

Exhibitionism   302.4
  Sexual Abuse Perpetrator

Fetishism   302.81
  Sexual Abuse Perpetrator

Frotteurism   302.89
  Sexual Abuse Perpetrator

**Generalized Anxiety
Disorder**   300.02
  Older Adult Abuse
  Sexual Abuse Victim (Child)

**Intermittent Explosive
Disorder**   312.34
  Alcohol Abuse/Dependence
  Assaultive Behavior
  Child Physical/Verbal Abuse
  Drug Abuse/Dependence
  Partner Abuse

Learning Disorder NOS   315.9
Juvenile Delinquency

Major Depressive Disorder   296.xx
Assault Victim
Employment Conflicts
Housing Inadequacies
Neglect of Child
Nutritional Risk/Food Insecurity
Poverty
Psychosis
Rape Victim
Truancy

**Major Depressive Disorder,
Single Episode**   296.2x
Older Adult Abuse
Older Adult Isolation
Prostitution
Sexual Abuse Victim (Child)
Suicide Attempt

**Major Depressive Disorder,
Recurrent**   296.3x
Prostitution
Suicide Attempt

**Maladaptive Health Behaviors
Affecting General Medical
Condition**   316
Physical/Cognitive Disability

Mild Mental Retardation   317
Neglect of Child

**Moderate Mental
Retardation**   318.0
Neglect of Child

**Narcissistic Personality
Disorder**   301.81
Sexual Abuse Perpetrator

**No Diagnosis or Condition
on Axis II**   V71.09
Alcohol Abuse/Dependence
Assaultive Behavior
Assault Victim
Employment Conflicts
Family Conflict
Foster Care Maladjustment (Child)
Homelessness

Housing Inadequacies
Juvenile Delinquency
Juvenile Runaway
Murder Victim's Family
Negative Peer Group (Adolescent)
Neglect of Child
Nutritional Risk/Food Insecurity
Partner Abuse
Physical/Cognitive Disability
Poverty
Prostitution
Psychosis
Rape Victim
Sexual Abuse Perpetrator
Sexual Abuse Victim (Child)
Suicide Attempt
Suicide Victim's Family
Teen Pregnancy
Truancy

Occupational Problem   V62.2
Employment Conflicts
Housing Inadequacies
Nutritional Risk/Food Insecurity
Poverty

**Oppositional Defiant
Disorder**   313.81
Foster Care Maladjustment (Child)
Juvenile Delinquency
Juvenile Runaway
Negative Peer Group (Adolescent)
Truancy

**Pain Disorder Associated With
Both Psychological Factors
and a General Medical
Condition**   307.89
Physical/Cognitive Disability

**Pain Disorder Associated with
Psychological Factors**   307.80
Physical/Cognitive Disability

**Panic Disorder With
Agoraphobia**   300.21
Truancy

**Panic Disorder Without
Agoraphobia**   300.01
Truancy

Paranoid Personality Disorder   301.0
Employment Conflicts
Housing Inadequacies
Legal Involvement
Nutritional Risk/Food Insecurity
Partner Abuse
Poverty

Parent–Child Relational Problem   V61.20
Juvenile Runaway
Negative Peer Group (Adolescent)
Teen Pregnancy
Truancy

Pedophilia   302.2
Sexual Abuse Perpetrator

Personality Disorder NOS   301.9
Family Conflict
Partner Abuse

Phase of Life Problem   V62.89
Homelessness

Physical Abuse of Child (Victim)   995.5
Child Physical/Verbal Abuse

Polysubstance Dependence   304.80
Alcohol Abuse/Dependence
Drug Abuse/Dependence
Juvenile Delinquency

Posttraumatic Stress Disorder   309.81
Alcohol Abuse/Dependence
Assault Victim
Drug Abuse/Dependence
Older Adult Abuse
Rape Victim
Sexual Abuse Victim (Child)

Psychotic Disorder NOS   298.9
Employment Conflicts
Housing Inadequacies
Neglect of Child
Nutritional Risk/Food Insecurity
Poverty

Relational Problem Related to a Mental Disorder or General Medical Condition   V61.9
Teenage Pregnancy

Schizoaffective Disorder   295.70
Homelessness
Psychosis

Schizoid Personality Disorder   301.20
Employment Conflicts
Housing Inadequacies
Nutritional Risk/Food Insecurity
Poverty

Schizophrenia   295.xx
Homelessness
Psychosis

Schizophrenia, Disorganized Type   295.10
Employment Conflicts
Homelessness
Housing Inadequacies
Nutritional Risk/Food Insecurity
Poverty

Schizophrenia, Paranoid Type   295.30
Employment Conflicts
Homelessness
Housing Inadequacies
Nutritional Risk/Food Insecurity
Poverty

Schizophrenia, Residual Type   295.60
Homelessness

Schizophrenia, Undifferentiated Type   295.90
Employment Conflicts
Homelessness
Housing Inadequacies
Nutritional Risk/Food Insecurity
Poverty

BIBLIOGRAPHY

American Psychiatric Association (1994). *Diagnostic and Statistical Manual of Mental Disorders.* 4th ed. Washington, DC: Author.

Azrin, N., and V. Besalel (1980). *Job Club Counselor's Manual.* Austin, TX: Pr. Ed.

Berghuis, D. J., and A. E. Jongsma, Jr. (2000). *The Severe and Persistent Mental Illness Treatment Planner.* New York: John Wiley & Sons.

Forgatch, M., and G. Patterson (1987). *Parents and Adolescents.* Eugene, OR: Castalia.

James, J., and R. Friedman (1988). *The Grief Recovery Handbook: The Action Program for Moving Beyond Death, Divorce, and Other Losses.* San Francisco: HarperCollins.

Johnson, V. (1980). *I'll Quit Tomorrow.* New York: Harper & Row.

Kasl-Davis, C. (1992). *Many Roads, One Journey.* New York: HarperCollins.

Kaye, D. (1991). *Family Rules: Raising Responsible Children.* New York: St. Martins.

Paleg, K. (1997). *Ten Things Every Parent Needs to Know.* Oakland, CA: New Harbinger.

Phelan, T. (1995). *1-2-3 Magic: Training Your Preschoolers and Preteens to Do What You Want.* Glen Ellyn, IL: Child Management, Inc.

Portman, J., and M. Stewart (1999). *Renter's Rights.* Berkeley, CA: Nolo Press.

Wachel, T., D. York, and P. York. (1982). *Toughlove.* Garden City, NJ: Doubleday.

Westberg, G. (1962). *Good Grief: A Constructive Approach to the Problem of Loss.* Philadelphia: Augsburg Fortress Press.

ABOUT THE DISK*

TheraScribe® 3.0 and 3.5 Library Module Installation

The enclosed disk contains files to upgrade your TheraScribe® 3.0 or 3.5 program to include the behavioral definitions, goals, objectives, and interventions from *The Social Work and Human Services Treatment Planner.*

Note: You must have TheraScribe® 3.0 or 3.5 for Windows installed on your computer in order to use *The Social Work and Human Services Treatment Planner* library module.

To install the library module, please follow these steps:

1. Place the library module disk in your floppy drive.
2. Log in to TheraScribe® 3.0 or 3.5 as the Administrator using the name "Admin" and your administrator password.
3. On the Main Menu, press the "GoTo" button, and choose the Options menu item.
4. Press the "Import Library" button.
5. On the Import Library Module screen, choose your floppy disk drive a:\ from the list and press "Go." Note: It may take a few minutes to import the data from the floppy disk to your computer's hard disk.
6. When the installation is complete, the library module data will be available in your TheraScribe® 3.0 or 3.5 program.

Note: If you have a network version of TheraScribe® 3.0 or 3.5 installed, you should import the library module one time only. After importing the data, the library module data will be available to all network users.

User Assistance

If you need assistance using this TheraScribe® 3.0 or 3.5 add-on module, contact Wiley Technical Support at:

Phone: 212-850-6753
Fax: 212-850-6800 (Attention: Wiley Technical Support)
E-mail: techhelp@wiley.com

---

*Note: This section applies only to the book with disk edition, ISBN 0-471-37742-2.

178

For information on how to install disk, refer to the **About the Disk** section on page 178.

*Note: This section applies only to the book with disk edition, ISBN 0-471-37742-2.

CPSIA information can be obtained at www.ICGtesting.com
Printed in the USA
BVOW001331020513

319645BV00005B/83/P